Wheelchair Wisdom

Awaken Your Spirit through Adversity

by Linda Noble Topf

To Michael
You make the world a better place
and me a richer person.

Nothing is precious except that part of you which is in other people
and that part of others that is in you. Up there, on high, everything is one.

-- Pierre Teilhard de Chardin

ENDORSEMENTS OF *WHEELCHAIR WISDOM*

"Wheelchair Wisdom *bears testimony to what Linda has learned and experienced—the importance of each of us being authentic to a higher self. It describes how, regardless of circumstances, each one of us can move through life in a creative way, using the simple skills that Linda has discovered.*"

Bernie Siegel, MD, world renowned author and inspirational speaker

"Within each of us, there is an essential quality of being that is creative, peaceful, and whole—known in religions and cultures worldwide as 'the essence of love.' Wheelchair Wisdom *holds a life affirming message, teaching that people or circumstances do not cause us conflict or distress. Instead, it is our own thoughts, feelings, and attitudes about people, events (or wheelchairs) that produce our struggle. Each moment of our lives is a moment of conscious choice. In this remarkable book, Linda Noble Topf gently offers her readers practical steps and sound advice that transform the conflict, fear, and separation that can easily dominate our lives.*"

James F. Twyman, bestselling author, *The Barn Dance, The Moses Code;* founder of Beloved Community

"Linda Noble Topf and I have known each other since the late 1960s when Electric Factory concerts were just getting started in the then sleepy city of Philadelphia. Linda was a student at Moore College of Art & Design, and I was an emerging concert promoter. In 1981, when she found out she had MS, she was smack in the middle of being the one of the creative forces behind Philadelphia's 300th Birthday Party and Century IV celebration. Linda is a survivor . . . she doesn't know what else to do but keep creating, loving, and

giving away her talent, her art, and her reason for living.
Wheelchair Wisdom *is a gift from someone who confronts, every day, the greatest obstacles one can imagine, yet always appreciates the opportunities that lie before her. This book delivers an extraordinary message that, quite probably, will change the way you look at your life."*

Larry Magid, renowned veteran concert promoter, Larry Magid Entertainment Group, Electric Factory Concerts

"If you face a challenge, or love someone that does, Linda Noble Topf opens up a whole new dimension. As someone who grew up with a mother who had MS, and who has tried to champion the cause of people to overcome all forms of disability for 40 years, I believe that Linda is writing a new and innovative chapter in the evolution of the greatest quest of all: living happily while staring down the realities of your life. Without fear, or trepidation, Linda's Wheelchair Wisdom: Awaken Your Spirit through Adversity *is an anthem for the new area of the able disabled. It's a book for everyone, not just the challenged, it is a story that will help all of us guide and comfort the people we care about with deep affection and a clearer understanding of their opportunities ahead. Linda's ideas are more than dreams – they are reality."*

Larry Kane, veteran author and anchorman, Vice Chair of the Greater Delaware Valley Chapter of the National MS Society.

"In her new book, Wheelchair Wisdom, *Linda Noble Topf shares how to take life to the next level and live it to the fullest – whatever the circumstances. It is an invaluable resource for people with MS, their family members and caregivers. Together they will explore how to trust and own their feelings and take responsibility for them in order to find freedom in their lives, once again. At Inglis, more than half our consumers have MS – dealing with it in its many*

manifestations. Wheelchair Wisdom is so informative because its story is told with clarity and truthfulness, with a generous dash of humor."

Gavin Kerr, President & CEO, Inglis House

"Ms. Linda Noble Topf serves as an inspiration to many with her profound ability to overcome difficult challenges and obstacles while fully embracing all that life has to offer with poise, dignity, and grace."

Renée Amoore, President and CEO, The Amoore Group, Inc., King of Prussia, PA

"Millions of men and women live with progressive MS, spinal cord injuries, and other health conditions that require utilization of wheelchairs and scooters to maintain independence and connection with their communities. If you or someone close to you is learning how to re-negotiate life from the perspective of limited mobility, Wheelchair Wisdom *is a must-read! This book outlines life tools and strategies in ten lessons, offering tips for managing the emotional ups and downs of everyday life by first finding the peace within yourself, regardless of what is happening to you on the outside. By acknowledging the unique needs and issues of not only MS patients, but all people in wheelchairs, Linda Noble Topf has done a service for all of us by writing* Wheelchair Wisdom.*"*

Tami Caesar, President, Greater Delaware Valley Chapter – National MS Society, Philadelphia, PA

"In the year 2000, Linda Noble Topf inspired and designed the "Inspirations" exhibit at the National Liberty Museum in Philadelphia. All of the heroes (both celebrities and ordinary

citizens) profiled in the exhibit had either physical, mental, or emotional challenges, making their significance all the greater because they had these obstacles and still achieved remarkable success in their lives, and made a difference. They believed they had a job to do—to change society's perception of the disability community. These people didn't whine; they acted. They didn't give in to despair; they created a new way of perceiving. They created a new conversation of possibility.

"I invite you to read and be inspired by Wheelchair Wisdom, *where Linda once again creates a new conversation, and conveys the message that lies at the heart of her convictions: that we are more than just people in wheelchairs."*

Irvin Borowsky, Founder and Chairman – The National Liberty Museum, Philadelphia, PA

"During the thirty years since Linda Noble Topf was diagnosed with multiple sclerosis, she has turned the limitations of illness into limitless opportunities for growth in relationships, intimacy, self-worth, gratitude, confidence, and creativity. In Wheelchair Wisdom, *she shares these discoveries in a way that will transform the lives of her readers—illuminating the possibilities open to all of us, to express joy in our power, freedom, self-expression, and peace of mind—whether living with an illness, confronting an injury, or embracing the aging process."*

Gerald G. Jampolsky, MD; and **Diane Cirincione, PhD,** authors of *A Mini Course for Life, Change Your Mind – Change Your Life, Love is the Answer,* and *Finding Our Way Home*

"Linda Noble Topf has been under my care for multiple sclerosis since 1983. She is courageous and wise, and I have always been impressed by her positive outlook, even under the harshest

circumstances. It would benefit any *reader—not just those in wheelchairs—to hear what she has to say.* Wheelchair Wisdom *holds a life-affirming message: Each moment of our lives is a moment of choice. The question is how to make the choices that are right for us. In this remarkable book, Linda Noble Topf gently guides her readers with practical steps and sound advice that will change intention into action."*

Jeffrey I. Greenstein, MD – Multiple Sclerosis Institute, Philadelphia, PA

"Some people regard a person bound to a wheelchair as a victim in need of constant care. Then there are those who recognize the sacredness of all life and the unique spiritual opportunities that can only be had by someone who spends much of their life in a wheelchair. I trust you are among the latter since you are interested in this jewel of a book. Believe me, your time within its pages will be time well spent."

H. Ronald Hulnick, Ph.D., President, University of Santa Monica; and co-author, *Loyalty to Your Soul: The Heart of Spiritual Psychology*

"Linda Noble Topf is an activist in the very best sense of that word— a leading advocate of freedom for patients and their families and an eloquent spokesperson for those living with chronic illness. Wheelchair Wisdom *is truly the culmination of her remarkable work and a gift to all those dealing with illness or loss of mobility. It is both inspirational and practical, infused with the spirit of a woman who has overcome numerous obstacles in her own life and willingly shares her discoveries with others."*

Robert Evans, founder of The Messenger Network

"Wheelchair Wisdom *delivers exactly what the title promises—a heartfelt expression of Linda's own journey with MS and the lessons she's learned along the way. The book is filled with practical answers to Linda's own guiding question: 'In this moment, despite it all, who do I choose to be?'"*

Marilee Adams, PhD, Author – *Change Your Questions, Change Your Life: 10 Powerful Tools for Life and Work*

WHEELCHAIR WISDOM
AWAKEN YOUR SPIRIT THROUGH ADVERSITY

iUniverse books may be ordered through booksellers or by contacting:

iUniverse
1663 Liberty Drive
Bloomington, IN 47403
www.iuniverse.com
1-800-Authors (1-800-288-4677)

Because of the dynamic nature of the Internet, any web addresses or links contained in this book may have changed since publication and may no longer be valid. The views expressed in this work are solely those of the author and do not necessarily reflect the views of the publisher, and the publisher hereby disclaims any responsibility for them.

Any people depicted in stock imagery provided by Thinkstock are models, and such images are being used for illustrative purposes only. Certain stock imagery © Thinkstock.

ISBN: 978-1-4917-4804-6 (sc)
ISBN: 978-1-4917-4805-3 (e)

Print information available on the last page.

iUniverse rev. date: 06/19/2019

CONTENTS

Part Two
Awakening Your Spirit

I AM NOT AFRAID TO BREAK THE RULES IF IT WOULD LEAD TO NEW IDEAS

Knowing others is wisdom; knowing yourself is Enlightenment.
-- Lao Tzu

PREFACE

Challenge Accepted, Multiple Sclerosis...I've Already Beaten You

Within each of us, there is an essential quality of being that is creative, peaceful and whole — known in religions and cultures worldwide as 'the essence of love.' Wheelchair Wisdom holds a life-affirming message, teaching us that people, or circumstances, do not cause conflict or distress, and showing us that overcoming adversity is inspirational. Instead, it is our own thoughts, feelings and attitudes about people, events (or wheelchairs) that produce our struggle. Each moment of our lives is a moment of conscious choice.

Throughout my first book, You Are Not Your Illness, I demonstrate to the reader that we are not our bodies, thoughts or emotions, but we are all observers (or we become more aware) of our bodies, emotions and thoughts.

Ultimately, each relationship you have with another person reflects the relationship you have with yourself. How well (or poorly) you get along with yourself will be directly mirrored by how quickly you come back to Self: to the centered space that resides within us all. You know - the part of us that is the still observer of our thoughts, emotions and experiences.

We all spend countless hours in front of the mirror reviewing our looks, focusing on our flaws and trying to create a perfect look…whatever that is. All of us are unique in our own right and mirror work gives us back that knowledge and wisdom.

What is mirror work? It's when you face yourself in the mirror, look into your eyes and say, "I Love You." You may even tear up when you experience the magnificence of your true Self. You may be surprised how this simple process can have a profound affect on your well-being, as its influence follows you throughout the day

In this second edition of my book, I gently offer readers practical steps and sound advice that transform the conflict, fear and separation that can easily dominate our lives.

This may sound silly, but when was the last time you looked at yourself in the mirror and said, "I Love You"? In this moment, despite it all, who do you choose to be?

Sit back, relax and enjoy yourself. This book delivers an extraordinary message that, quite probably, will change the way you look at your life.

FOREWORD
by Dr. Daniel Gottlieb

After spending nearly a year in the hospital following my accident in 1979, I arrived home in my brand new power wheelchair at my brand new rental ranch house. Wanting to explore my new environment, I found myself trying to navigate through an expansive front yard in the new chair. After just a few minutes, however, my front tire got stuck in a gopher hole.

Naturally, I hollered for someone in the house to rescue me, but my voice was too weak, and no one heard me. I became frightened and continued to do the best I could to scream. Still no response. And then, out of fear and frustration, I began to cry and started banging on the sides of my wheelchair. After a few minutes of banging, I noticed my hands were bleeding so I stopped, exhausted and hopeless.

I just sat in silence for a few minutes, not even thinking. And that's when I noticed the birds were singing, and it was a beautiful autumn day. That day, I woke. I awoke to the fact that there was something going on besides my broken body and my crippled ego.

The twelfth step in The Twelve Steps of Alcoholics Anonymous starts with "Having had a spiritual awakening..." The first time I read that was in the early 1980s, when I joined Alcoholics Anonymous because I was dealing with substance abuse in my family. When I thought again about that phrase, I thought, "Yes, we have spiritual awakenings. But then we go back to sleep again. And if we are lucky, we have another awakening."

Over the course of these 30 years, I've had many awakenings; and it seems each time I have one, I am able to stay awake longer. As I look back over these 30 years, I have lived with quadriplegia, substance abuse in the family, divorce, the deaths of my ex-wife, my beloved sister, and both of my parents. I have faced my own death several times—the most recent being a few months ago. And despite—or because of—all of these awakenings, I am more content, grateful, and loving than I could have ever imagined. And how did I get here? I'm not really sure, but here's what I think.

I've learned about the futility of fighting with my body, and even fighting *for* my body. I've learned that compassion changes everything. When we suffer, we need compassion—we need someone who can look in our eyes, understand our suffering, and be there with us. When my body suffers, my body needs compassion. So when my body suffers with pain, or urinary tract infections, or spasms, I feel great sadness and compassion for this body that suffers. I feel compassion for this body that has worked so hard for so many years to enable me to live this precious life.

So I no longer fight with my body; I care for it with love. And I am less inclined to be self-critical or judgmental. After all, my mind is my mind, and it also needs compassion when it is racing or scared or depressed. It does not need harsh judgment.

So we awaken and go back to sleep. We release our grasp and open up to the world and to our lives; and then our hearts close, and we clutch to anything that gives us the illusion of security. We realize that wheelchairs and walkers and broken bodies are not who we are, that who we are is about fortitude and resilience and love of life. And then something happens, and we are back to being patients or powerless or handicapped.

What I could have used (and probably could still use) is a gentle guide who could take my hand and show me how to open up to my life, slowly and lovingly. This gentle guide would show me how to find compassion for others when they suffer, and to find it for myself when I suffer. And most important, I wish someone had taught me how to experience the life I have with grace and gratitude, rather than resenting what I've lost and wishing for some future vision.

This gentle guide is Linda Noble Topf and in writing this book, she takes your hand...

-- Dr. Daniel Gottlieb

My barn having burned to the ground, I can now see the moon.
--Japanese folk saying

ACKNOWLEDGMENTS

I am grateful for the teachings of Spirit that are woven throughout the pages of this book. They have been manifested through my spiritual teachers, John-Roger and John Morton, and find their way into my heart and into this work. I am forever grateful for their presence in my life and for their guidance in bringing Wheelchair Wisdom forward into the Light.

I am blessed to be surrounded by many amazing intelligent and wise people who have respected me and my work, and providing me with their gifted guidance. Thank you to all of you—my friends, colleagues and business associates—who have been involved on my path to mastership.

First and foremost, thanks to Ed Claflin, who has been my writing coach and alter ego throughout the process of bringing this book into existence. He has been its guardian angel with his gentle, perceptive criticism, which has been essential to the quality of the finished product. He has been totally committed to the 'wisdoms' contained herein becoming a spiritual primer for those on the path to higher consciousness. Thank you, Ed, for your belief in me. I understand now that finding my voice was, indeed, like climbing a mountain. And because of your unwavering commitment and insight, I was empowered to complete the upward climb to the top. Every writer should be lucky enough to have Ed by his or her side.

My deepest gratitude to Judi Leventhal, my office assistant,— and key to all my endeavors—who did much to bring the book to completion. She put in countless hours of creative and loyal support—writing, editing, and proofreading—offering insightful suggestions for clarification that proved heartfelt and helpful. Without her, this book would not have been possible.

And for their steadfast empowerment, thanks to my friends Marilee Adams, Kim Aubry and Elizabeth Frumin for checking in on me weekly with love and concern. They all gently guided me back home—to the source of love, beauty, and grace that comes from within.

With their commitment, honesty and appreciation, my professional "home team" made it all possible. My heartfelt thanks goes to Dan Gottlieb, PhD, for his support and trust; and also to Susan Critelli, Terry Andrews, Traci Anderson, Johanna Vonderling, Gary Green, Larry Keller, Jeffrey Greenstein, MD; and Serge Goldberg, my vigilant physical trainer for more than fifteen years. I am deeply grateful for their unflinching emotional support. They always remind me that my word in the world is a reflection of my determination, and a commitment to my purpose.

To all those who have supported the evolutionary process of the book coming into existence:

Crucial to any creative work is the ongoing support of teachers, peers, and mentors. In invaluable ways, each of these individuals, whose integrity and belief in me I cherish, have made a notable difference for me: Renee Amoore, The Amoore Group; Russell Bishop, Creator – Insight Seminars; Irv Borowsky, Founder, The National Liberty Museum; Tami Caesar, President, Greater

Delaware Valley Chapter of The National MS Society; Robert Evans, Founder, The Messenger Network; Jeffrey Greenstein, M.D., Greenstein Neurology; Arianna Huffington, Chair, President, and Editor-in-Chief, The Huffington Post Media Group; Drs. Ron and Mary Hulnick, Designers and Founding Faculty of the University of Santa Monica's Master's Degree Programs in Spiritual Psychology; Jerry G. Jampolsky, M.D., and Diane Cirincione, Ph.D., Attitudinal Healing International; Larry Kane, Veteran Newscaster and Author; Gavin Kerr, M.D., President/CEO, Inglis House; Kevin McGuire, AbleRoad; Bernie S. Siegel, M.D., Author, *Love, Medicine and Miracles*; and James F. Twyman, Author, *The Barn Dance* and The Moses Code, and Peter T. Wilderotter, President CEO, Christopher and Danna Reeve Foundation.

Arianna Huffington and me
IMAGE COURTESY OF DEVID KELLY CROW

From my heart, for the fellowship and loving we share in Spirit, I acknowledge all of you.

I am deeply grateful to my delightful circle of friends for their ongoing love and support: Helene Aronberg; Mel Barton; Michele Benjamin; Mitch Blatstein; Glenn Cooper, M.D.; Barrett Cordero of BigSpeak, Inc.; David Cunningham; Jeff DeLone; Karen Dempsey; Barb DiSippio; Nicky Faeth of BigSpeak. Inc.; Joan Geller; Michael Hayes; Arlene Kaufman; Don & Karen Kaufman; Marlyn Kline; Joan Kurkian; Carol Giges Moskovitz; Dawn & Albert Mazzone; Kevin McGuire of AbleRoad; Cubby Moreland; Lee Nelson; Cathy Nierenberg; Dani Noble; Pete Pajil; Bob Penneys; Sabrina Quairoli; Ali Randall; Cindy Ratzlaff; Audrey Reed; Trudy Shuman; Gary & Shary Skoloff; Marianne Sladzinski; Roger Smith; Shanda Sumpter; Robert Toporek; Eve West; Jonathan Wygant of BigSpeak, Inc.; Lala Zeitlyn; My Facebook Friends; and The Huffington Post Staff.

And to my spiritual family in the Movement of Spiritual Inner Awareness: You have guided me through the darkness and held me in my pain. My gratitude is deep.

Thanks, too, to every person living a life of challenge who has supported himself/herself by reading my first book, You Are Not Your Illness: Seven Principles for Meeting the Challenge; reading/commenting on my monthly articles on Huffington Post; and attending my webinars, groups and lectures over the years. Your inspiration has given me continual courage and upliftment. You know who you are.

Special heartfelt thanks to my parents, Rita and Marvin Noble; my brother, Stuart; Michael's parents, Muriel and Ernie Topf; and to my cousin, Lottie Plaut, who all celebrate this book from another place.

For her steadfast and loving empowerment, I thank my niece, Dani, who gave me the encouragement and humility needed to complete this work. And to Shary and Gary Skoloff, my sister-in-law and brother-in-law. Thank you for being a loving presence, whenever I called you for reassurance and upliftment.

And lastly, my deepest gratitude goes to Michael Topf, my husband, muse and best friend, with whom I share my life. You are a daily expression of the highest manifestation of love. Thank you for your faith in me, for what we have learned together, and for making this all possible. I love you with all my heart.

And finally, the depth of my gratitude is to the Divine Guidance that alone makes this and all works possible.

Introduction:
What Is Wheelchair Wisdom?

It's a truism that a journey of a thousand miles begins with a single step. For some of us, though, that first step is a classified ad in a magazine.

I placed that ad in *Philadelphia* magazine back in 1984, about three years after I had first been diagnosed with MS. I was not yet wheelchair bound, but knew I would be. I had been given a diagnosis that told me my life would be shorter than I anticipated—but how much shorter? I had been told that my disease was incurable, that there were no breakthroughs on the horizon—drugs, therapies, or palliatives—but I had no knowledge of the research and only the sketchiest understanding of the way MS would affect my nerves, my brain, and my ability to function.

Looking back, I can also see that I was making my way through those emotional states that Elisabeth Kübler-Ross has labeled the "stages of grief": denial, anger, bargaining, depression, and acceptance. Though Kübler-Ross based her observations on her interactions with dying patients, she also observed that these "stages" apply to many other circumstances—for instance when we experience loss of income, loss of freedom, the death of a loved one, or the onset of disease or chronic illness. She also observed that there was no preordained order to these stages of grieving. What she described was a roller-coaster effect. Years later, when I read of her research, I was struck by just how accurately she had defined what I went through then—all the stages, but in no particular order. And how long was I caught up in each stage? I can't say—but I know that I was in the grip of that all-encompassing experience of grieving.

How did I deal with it? Somehow I just kept going, meeting each day as it came, by force of habit. And not all of those habits were productive or even healthy. I was a chronic cigarette smoker. My diet was a thoughtless amalgam of snacks, "easy-to-prepare meals," caffeinated and alcoholic drinks. I had drugs—both prescription and otherwise—that could bring me up or down, calm my nerves, deaden my feelings, and help me get through the hours of the day and night.

Clearly, my disease was ruling my life. I was in its control. And yet as the days, weeks, and months passed without any drastic changes in my health or abilities, I began to realize just how little I understood this thing called MS that was taking over my life and riveting my attention. What *was* the status of the research? Where *were* studies being done? What avenues were being explored by doctors, scientists, and health practitioners, and what were they learning? And what about all those people who had already been diagnosed with MS—well over a quarter of a million in the U.S. alone? What had they learned about coping with the disease? What knowledge did they have that they could share, possibly making life better for all of us who were part of this community?

Soon my newfound sense of hope began to find ways to manifest itself in my work. It was in October of 1984 that I placed that classified ad in *Philadelphia* magazine asking if anyone else who had MS was interested in attending a conference I was thinking of putting together—a conference to support others like me who were dealing with MS. I believed we would all benefit from educating ourselves on alternative treatments and from sharing practical information, strategies, and tips to deal with this unpredictable disease. Most of all, I wanted to begin to establish a community and build a network of support for all of us.

I started to get a few phone calls in response to my ad. I had no plan and no idea what such a conference would cover, but I started by making a call to reserve a room in which to hold it. I put together a black-and-white flyer saying, "Find out about attitudes and alternatives for dealing with MS," announcing a November conference. Michael and I drove around Philadelphia putting the flyer up all over Center City.

Fueled by the desire to help myself as well as other people facing what I was facing, I got to work contacting alternative practitioners from as far away as England and Scotland to come to the conference to discuss a range of topics, things like mercury toxicity, the relationship between dairy products and MS, the value of stretching and yoga, macrobiotics, shiatsu massage, and barometric oxygen therapy. This was in 1984, an era when doctors were treated as gods, and exploring treatments on your own was a very radical concept. Still, more than ninety people showed up to find out how they could take a more active role in dealing with their illness. The seminars covered a wide range of topics—alternative treatments, nutrition and exercise, self-expression, sexuality, stress, motivation, spirituality, and caregivers.

The conference was a great success. I was thrilled by the response, the turnout, and the level of engagement of everyone who came. Participants were able to reconnect with the power they had always had—instead of just being labeled by an illness. They began to rediscover, reclaim, and redefine what it really means to be alive. It was wonderful! Doors had been opened, connections had been made. We had broken down many of the barriers that exist between practitioners and patients. All of us were equals in this new dialog. Here were the beginnings of what, truly, was a community, and I expected that the lines of communication that had been opened up, and the sense of mission that I felt, would continue long after the conference was over.

But something else had happened too. There had been a change in me. I remember standing on the street outside the conference hall at the end of the day, so happy the event was over and that it had gone so well. A creature of habit, I did exactly what I usually did on these occasions. The pressure was off. There was a reason to celebrate. So…I lit a cigarette. Inhaled deeply. Again. And again.

And then—I looked at the cigarette in my hand. *What was I doing?* Here I was, conference over, puffing away. And what had we just talked about during this conference? Repeatedly, the discussions had circled back to key themes. That we were, each one of us, responsible for our actions and our behavior. We could choose to eat healthful diets that would give us strength and stamina—or we could choose foods that contributed to obesity, heart disease, and other chronic health problems (besides the huge one we already had!). We had the freedom to take medications or refuse them. And those of us who were chronic smokers, hooked on nicotine, dependent on a habit that was proven to be carcinogenic—well, it was a choice. I could keep on. Or I could give it up. Wasn't that what I had just learned?

I stopped smoking a week after that.

***

We are constantly invited to be who we are.
-- Henry David Thoreau

***

I dubbed my project "The MS Initiative." As I had hoped, this first event turned out to be far more than a conference where everyone took notes and then went home to resume their lives just as before. Instead, we had started something that felt unstoppable. Support groups, organized by people who had met at the conference, began meeting monthly—giving participants the opportunity to share what they'd learned, report on their personal successes and failures, and above all, be with others who understood or shared their experiences and feelings. We launched a newsletter. We set up a budget and began doing fund-raising to publicize the aims of the MS Initiative and expand the number of groups that began meeting throughout Pennsylvania and nearby states. I remember driving to

New York City and Washington, DC, monthly, and also flying to Boston monthly, to lead seminars.

Soon we were discussing the idea of having a weekend retreat—something that I don't think had ever been tried before in the MS community. At first it looked as if the challenges were insurmountable. Where would we find a camp with facilities that were accessible to all of us? How would we accommodate people with many different ranges of mobility, ensuring the access and the health facilities that we would need? Almost miraculously, one by one, we dealt with the difficulties and resolved them; and in June of 1986, we had our first weekend summer retreat at Appel Farm, an arts and music center in Elmer, New Jersey. It was a huge success, leading to more retreats in the summers to come. (As one participant wrote afterwards, "I haven't felt this good since I was diagnosed. The camp proved to me that *I could do it!*")

Meanwhile, we pursued our goals of organizing more conferences and support groups and disbursing information for family members in Pennsylvania and other states. As I empowered myself and others to have hope, I discovered that sense of freedom that has stayed with me ever since. I didn't know what my future would hold, but I was regaining my faith that I could affect it. I refused to accept that I would become a hapless victim of a dreaded disease. I was still angry that MS had come into my life, but I had come to realize that my rage was a very powerful force, and that, underneath it, my will to live was asserting itself.

I knew what I was, and was not, going to do. I *was not* going to resign myself to being a pitiful cripple waiting for death. I *was* going to embrace my life and do whatever I could to live my life as fully as possible.

I was just beginning to see glimmers of the spiritual transformation that my MS diagnosis would bring, a powerful shift that would sweeten my views on aging, change, and the challenges each of us must ultimately face. In the years that followed, multiple sclerosis would teach me how to love more deeply than I'd ever dreamed I could. It woke me up, dissolved any illusions that I had control over my life, forced me to slow down, and brought me back home to myself. I began to take more responsibility for the choices I made in my life. I learned that no matter what was happening to my body, I was in charge of how I responded. I no longer wanted to just react, unthinking, to what was happening to me. I wanted to make a conscious decision to take action and stand up for what I believed in.

And what had become of my own grieving? It continued…as, in a sense, I'm sure it always will. Certainly, there was the denial. Every time I heard about a possible breakthrough that seemed to promise a remission or a cure, I sought it out. I tried alternative medicine, herbal therapy. I took trips to Mexico to meet with practitioners who claimed they had found the secret to a cure; and I went to South Dakota and spent three weeks at a Lakota Sioux reservation participating in their ceremonies and sweat lodges. I kept trying new diets and went long months avoiding certain foods—trying anything, *anything* that promised new hope. I would begin to see improvements, and then—once again—I would have a relapse, or my symptoms would worsen, each cycle producing new symptoms of grief with its components of depression, anger, and bargaining. But gradually, at first with great pain and later with increasing joy, I moved toward the stage that helped me move ahead, to see a future, to *have* a future—the stage of acceptance.

To many, I think, the word "acceptance" has negative connotations—implying compliance, resignation, submission, even victimization. To me its meaning is completely the opposite. In acceptance there is freedom—release from the anger and frustration that we feel when a promised cure fails to work or a thread of hope suddenly snaps. With acceptance comes renewal—the ability to live in the present and experience the possibilities of each moment. Acceptance doesn't mean that we *stop feeling* or *put on a happy face*. Quite the opposite. It means that we own our feelings—the petulance and frustration when we drop something or forget something; the deep sorrow when we lose some of our mobility or recall our former lives; the joy of being with loved ones, sharing a moment, or making new discoveries. We can't accept some without accepting all—because all those emotions, and others that are impossible to name, are part of who we are.

With acceptance comes a new perspective. What matters is not what we were, what we lost, or what might happen in the future. What matters is the *now*. For example, when I first started using a cane to help me walk, it showed me a new perspective on the simple act of walking. To move forward, I now had to be aware of the movement of my legs and feet. I had to shift my weight to my heel, lean forward, roll toward my toes, then shift weight to my other heel, lean forward, and roll toward my toes. Heel, roll, toes . . . heel, roll, toes. Walking became slow and methodical. I had to be aware of several things: What was the landscape like? Where was the crack in the sidewalk, the bump or incline in the pavement? Slowing down and focusing on the simplicity of the act forced me to view my surroundings with new eyes.

Looking back, I realize how important that forming the MS Initiative and holding that first conference were in helping me to open up so many new perspectives. The conference was such a pivotal event that I now find it impossible to imagine what my life would have been like without it. Looking back at it now, I realize it was far more than just a conference. It was truly the initiation of something that had not existed before. It established a link for a community that desperately needed one, and lasting bonds among those who took part.

What was it like for others? Afterward, I heard from Joel Raffel, one of the participants. His message is eloquent:

> *"I started to realize there was more to be gotten from my life. It gave me hope, strength, and the support that I was looking for. My future started to look clearer in my mind. I came away from the Initiative with the feeling there is strength in numbers. I am not my illness, but the way I deal with it shapes my disease and how I deal with it."*

What changed our perspectives? I doubt that the formation of the MS Initiative made any lasting contribution to the progress of research (though there were many topics we discussed—such as nutrition, menopause, exercise/fitness, attitudinal healing—that are now recognized to be very important indeed!) But what really made a difference was the discovery that while each of us was living with a disease, we were not that disease. *You Are Not Your Illness* would become the title of my first book—a title summarizing everything that evolved from the MS Initiative. All of us were *living with* MS. None of us had *become* MS. We needed to recognize it, know more about it. Perhaps there would be new discoveries (there were!), and new medications (there would be), and new ways to deal with our limitations (how grateful I am for today's technology!). But our lives did not depend on these developments. Our lives were *our own*—not our disease's—and each of us could determine what to do with ourselves.

This, to me, is the universal part of *Wheelchair Wisdom*. It is what has become the theme of my work—and of the chapters ahead. Now…I want to share with you what I've learned these past thirty years. In the pages that follow, you'll "walk" with me through illuminating steps that will offer you the opportunity to dissolve, shift, and reinvent worn out beliefs—moving from the thought "we *are* our bodies and our perceived limitations" (the essence of who we are is greater than that!) to a more forgiving, compassionate, and peaceful practice of embracing the view that "we are *not* our bodies, or our body image." This book will introduce a new vision of possibility and gratitude in order to move forward on a path of fulfillment in your remaining time on the planet.

I have written Wheelchair Wisdom: Awaken Your Spirit through Adversity to identify and define the character traits of acceptance, courage, creativity, connection, empathy, giving back, and gratitude (among others) that I hope will empower my passionate generation and others to shift their perceptions about aging, retirement, and death. It is my hope that anyone who reads this book will use this new ideology to continue to live a joyful, fulfilling life well into their fifties, sixties, seventies, and beyond.

This book, too, is an initiative, in the strongest meaning of that word. I hope you and I will initiate new thoughts, actions, and perspectives. Whether you are in any stage of grieving, or have moved to acceptance, the initiative is yours. Your new journey may begin for you, as it did for me, with whatever first step you need to take. It could be something as simple as taking out an ad in a magazine. A conversation. An email message. A phone call. Or … turning to the next page of this book …

Finish each day and be done with it. For you have done what you could.
Tomorrow is a new day; begin it well and serenely and
with too high a spirit to be encumbered with your old nonsense.
-- Ralph Waldo Emerson

While here, love what is here.
Have no issue with anything or anyone.
Choose unconditional love.
Make no demands.
Love anyway.
Love if you do.
Love if you don't.
Love when it is dark.
Love when it is light.
Just love.
-- John Morton, *You Are the Blessings*

Part One
Finding Your True Self

Honoring Our Word

My husband Michael loves martial arts. On Saturday mornings, he has a martial arts class that he looks forward to all week. Recognizing this, I have made it my responsibility to make sure that I get home care coverage on Saturday morning so he can get to his martial arts on time.

In my world, that's just one of the things that I'm responsible for. But in any given week, it might be difficult to arrange for coverage on a Saturday morning. Or I might be feeling low, and would much rather have Michael by my side than a home-care person. He does so much for me, during so many days and nights. But ultimately, I have to be responsible for making sure Michael takes care of himself, because if I fall short on this commitment, he cannot be responsible to me.

This is not a rule that we've created. It's not an obligation for us. It's simply a habit that we have made part of our lives—just one example of the habit of integrity that I try to practice every day.

I begin with the habit of integrity because I believe it's the underpinning and the foundation of all the other habits of wheelchair wisdom.

Fundamentally, it's easy enough to understand what we mean by integrity. It means being true to yourself.

That might seem clear and simple. But to make a *habit* of integrity requires something else of us. It requires discipline.

I realize that may seem abstract, which is why I gave the example of Michael and me and our understanding about Saturday mornings. To begin with, we love each other (more than words can say!) and we have been married for many years. Early in our marriage—before I had MS and before he became the partner looking after so much of my care—it would have supremely simple for him to say, "I want to go to a martial arts class every Saturday morning." How easy! He would go to martial arts, I'd put in some additional work at my design firm (which I loved doing), or see to some housework, or catch up with friends and family. These are the kinds of trade-offs that partners negotiate frequently, and it works out well as long as both are honest about what they want to do and mutually considerate of the other person's needs.

But now… consider that relationship reconfigured with one of the partners in a wheelchair. She needs help getting out of bed and dressed in the morning. She has limited mobility around the house, and it takes her extra time to do everything. This means, while Michael is enjoying himself at martial arts on a Saturday morning, she will need a caretaker just to help manage her basic needs.

What should they do now? (And remember, they very much love each other!) Michael could say to himself, "It's really not fair for me to be away on Saturday mornings. I work during the week, Linda needs help on the weekend, getting a caretaker to come is extra expense and hassle, and maybe I won't miss my martial arts class after all." On my side, I could be saying, "I didn't ask to be an invalid; it's not my fault that I'm in a wheelchair, and you can't act like everything is the way it was before."

My question is, where is the *integrity* in a discussion like that? Where are we, if Michael tries to deny his love of martial arts and convince himself that he doesn't deserve those Saturday mornings? How am I being true to my love for Michael if I act like a victim who can't do anything for herself and must always rely on him for help? That's not Michael! That's not me!

The truth is so much more complicated than that, and to get at that truth means we both have to act with integrity. He needs to tell me about his love for martial arts and how important it is to his physical and emotional well-being. (If he denied that, if he lied about it, just think how he'd be betraying himself!) I need to tell him that I'm not a helpless victim, that I can take care of myself with the help of a caretaker, and I'm perfectly capable of lining up someone to come in while he's away. (If I said otherwise, I'd be pretending to be more helpless than I am.) Once we have spoken our truths and recognized our needs, everything else becomes possible. I honor my word—to the best of my ability—to make arrangements for coverage every Saturday morning. Michael honors his commitment—to the best of his ability—to get to martial arts.

Being True to Your Feelings

Above all, the habit of integrity means making a promise to yourself that you will be responsible for every moment in your life. Inevitably, there are times when we say to ourselves, "I don't want to..." But if we've made a promise to ourselves to be responsible for what we do, we can't listen to that voice. We are responsible for every single moment: ultimately, each of us chooses how we want to live.

If you are in a wheelchair, living with chronic illness, or dealing with the limitations of an aging body, I think you are completely familiar with the emotions that we feel when we experience our losses. I vividly recall how I felt when I began to lose mobility. It was shocking, depressing, frustrating, infuriating. I wanted to cry, yell, rant, rave, and turn my back on the world. When I gradually began to lose the use of my hands and legs—and physical therapy and recovery seemed agonizingly slow—I reacted with rage. When my limbs and reflexes deteriorated to the point that I lost my ability to drive—and I lost the independence that goes with that—the unfairness of it all nearly overwhelmed me. I felt cheated when I couldn't clap or snap my fingers to Stevie Wonder's music, much less dance to it with Michael (which had always been one of our favorite things to do together). And when I saw people bicycling, running, or taking long walks, I felt deep jealousy. Even today, my envy and longing can be triggered when I see others doing what I can no longer do. There's so much they don't have to worry about—

4

fatigue, spasms, frequent bathroom trips, and all the problems of accessibility—impossible stairways, few access ramps, sidewalks with high curbs, narrow doorways…I could go on and on.

Yes, I own all these feelings—and at times they are in the forefront of my consciousness. I can't plaster over those feelings with a list of cautions and reminders about how I *should* feel. A façade of good cheer is not the answer. Putting a smile on your face when you're suffering inside is like putting a cork in the top of a volcano. The anger is real. The heartbreak is real. And those feelings won't be denied. If you try to pretend they don't exist, they'll make their presence known one way or another, perhaps in resentment toward people and situations that have little to do with the real issues, or in emotional outbursts when you least expect them. (We've learned that suppressed emotions can even make you physically ill.) If we try to hide or deny some of our emotions, labeling them as "negative," there's a good chance that we'll suppress *all* our feelings. Then what becomes of the positive emotions—enthusiasm, joy, happiness, and love—that are also part of our lives?

I know what it's like when you attempt to annihilate the range of feelings that you experience. After I was diagnosed with MS, there were days and weeks when I tried to bury my feelings in a haze of drugs and alcohol. Things began to change for me when I started listening inwardly to my newly awakening heart. I learned to become much more accepting of myself and others than I had ever been. Yes, I put a lot of effort into trying alternative treatments that I hoped would improve my health, but I had to admit that I couldn't simply fix myself with more vitamin B or organic tofu in my diet, or with the latest steroid treatment for MS.

The only way to truly move beyond the heartache and anger of facing life in a wheelchair is to accept all of your emotions—own them, know them, experience them. That's integrity. Feelings of *all kinds* will express themselves. That doesn't change, just because you're in a wheelchair. They continue to rise up and flow through you. There's no way to bury them or deny they exist. But you can *let them go.*

Responsibility

Have you ever been angry at someone?

What a ridiculous question.

Of course you have. We all have. But now let me take it one step further and ask you, "Have you ever been angry at someone and *decided not to let that person know?*"

Again, I'm sure your answer is "Yes." Denying or hiding our feelings is as common as *having* those feelings, and most of us are pretty good at rationalizing why we do it. We might be saying (to ourselves), "I don't want this person to know—or *their* feelings may be hurt." Or: "I know I'm angry but I have no right to be angry because of all this person has done for me in the past." Or it could get even more complicated than that: "This person thinks of me as a calm and patient friend (or spouse, or partner), and if I let them know I'm angry, I'll ruin the glue that holds our relationship together."

The feeling that you start with—in this case, anger—is not at all messy. It's natural, it's human, it might even be numbered among our most common emotions. But all the "stuff" that comes afterward? Hiding your anger? Denying it? Making up hyper-rational reasons why your spouse or child or parent or partner or friend or lover should never know? All that gets messy. Very messy.

Let's look closely at what happens, and I think you'll see why. Let's say you're angry at your spouse when you part from each other in the morning. Reasonably enough, you decide not to express your anger right away because you're both facing the day's obligations, you have places to go and things to do. But then let's further suppose that anger bounces around in you during the day, so from time to time you're thinking, "When are we going to talk about this?" and then a little later, "*Should* we even discuss it?" and, maybe sometime after lunch or when you begin to look forward to going home, "I should skip it. Let it slide. I don't want to make an issue of it. Maybe this is all about nothing."

What I've just described—that kind of inner dialog—is all a transition toward messiness. Look how you started out, feeling a clear emotion that was just an emotion. Then you walked out the door and put the emotion in a separate compartment, and that's when things started to happen. You began to wonder whether your emotion was valuable or important enough to "reveal" at some later time. You thought about the ways the discussion or revelation of your anger could have an impact on the relationship—what might or might not happen if you brought it up. Perhaps you began to formulate what you believed would be your spouse's reply to you, or you replayed a previous "script" to help you decide whether to talk about your anger. Or you began playing it over again and again in your mind until you decided, "I don't have the energy for this, so why bring it up?"

So you get home. You begin the evening, and then we all know what happens. You get agitated or annoyed or impatient at something completely unrelated or irrelevant to your buried, compartmentalized, and stored-away (you thought!) source of anger.

What a mess.

Been there? Done that? I'm sure. We all have. We end up wishing we could press "rewind," go back to the beginning, and just *own* that emotion when it was still clear and unadorned—before things got so messy.

So far, I've been describing a situation that any two people in a relationship could get into. But just consider (as if you don't already know!) when one partner is in a wheelchair or in frequent need of care and attention. Even more messiness! If I'm the cared-for person, I could begin saying things to myself like, "I can never be angry: I owe so much to so many people for taking care of me." Or: "I'm not angry about something, I'm angry about everything—this wheelchair, my limitations, my dependence, my incapacity." And the emotion, the anger that is mine, that I feel passing through me, becomes a quantity that I weigh on an internal scale as I try to decide, "Should I feel it? Do I *deserve* to feel it? Do I have a *right?* Am I *worthy* of feeling it? Is it too *much?*"

And there it is again: that messiness.

So…how do we take responsibility for clearing up the mess?

The Choices We Make

I believe we can make choices that allow our emotions to *flow*. I'm not saying it's easy to let rage course through your body, or look fear in the eye, or feel that place inside where your heart is broken. But you can make some choices that help you take responsibility for your emotions rather than waging the tough battle of trying to keep your feelings at bay.

1. Observe the timing and rhythm of your emotions.

It's very easy and natural to get so immersed in your feelings that you feel as though you *are* your emotions. We all do it, and it's one of the reasons they have so much power over us. But the truth is, emotions are something *you have*—they come and they go, and they are separate from you. Remember, who you are is *not* your emotions.

You can develop the ability to gain enough objective distance by observing the rise and fall of your emotions with a degree of detachment, almost as though you were watching an event happening to someone else. I call this *awareness*. Imagine a large magnifying glass on the reality of what you're feeling. Give those emotions a chance to come to the surface and be seen. If they flow through you, you "gain altitude" on those feelings. Their grip on you will become less and less strong over time. You can never expect your core feelings to go away. There may always be moments when the reality of your situation hits you between the eyes and it just takes your breath away. But in time you'll be able to diffuse the energy of those feelings as you learn to acknowledge and release them without getting stuck in them.

2. Take a breath. Give yourself permission to step outside yourself and observe yourself.

Whatever your behavior looks like on the outside, there are most likely painful emotions lurking deep inside. They need to be acknowledged. I find there are many situations, for someone in a wheelchair, where these emotions are stirred up. When you encounter the rude stare, the insensitive waiter, the public restroom door that's too small for your wheelchair, the handicapped parking space abused by those who are "just going in for a minute"—what are your feelings? These feelings are apt to be triggered on a daily basis. And they can reignite the flame of that initial anger and grief about your loss of mobility. You can't stop these emotions from arising. But can you let them move through you without dictating your response to the situation? If you can, you'll be better able to move through your days with grace, dignity, and calmness.

3. Be aware of any judgment you have about yourself. When you are in confusion or doubt, be still, and listen inwardly for guidance.

Your feelings cannot be labeled or judged. There is no such thing as a "bad" emotion. Your feelings just *are*. Notice any judgment you carry about yourself as these feelings come up. Try to let go of that judgment and simply accept each emotion as a message from deep inside.

When you label anger, sadness, resentment or any other emotion as an enemy—or a sign of some failing on your part—you set up a cycle of resistance that actually gives the emotion more power over you. For example, if you believe it's wrong to be angry and you label your anger as a "negative" emotion that needs to be hidden, it will simmer and stew inside you until it makes you sick or depressed or erupts at some future point when you least expect it. Remember, what you resist, *persists.*

The truth is that emotions are a fundamental part of who we are. They give us valuable information about how to conduct our lives—how to find work that is meaningful, avoid people who would do us harm, learn more effective ways to accomplish a task, or just enjoy a beautiful day. I know there are probably moments when you wish you could just numb the ability to feel, so you wouldn't have to "deal with" emotions. But it never hurts to remind ourselves that a life without feeling would be a life filled with apathy, ruled by carelessness. And I'm sure none of us wants to live like that.

4. Ask for support.

I've always been very independent, determined to do things on my own, and have never been one to ask for help. MS forced me to learn that accepting support when I need it isn't a sign of weakness, but can in fact be a real gift for me—and a sign of strength, and an opportunity to authentically connect with others. And something more: my asking for support can also be a gift for the person who is giving it to me (whether they realize it or not).

Talking with someone you trust about your feelings may be one of the most healing things you can do. A compassionate word or touch, or a tender smile from someone who cares about you will help draw you out of the dark place where the emotions can feel so overwhelming. And just knowing there's someone who knows how to listen, who cares enough to really try to understand, can go a long way to relieve your sense of isolation.

It may be difficult to think of baring your heart. I'm sure you are feeling some things that you have difficulty admitting to yourself, let alone anyone else. But here's some wheelchair wisdom: the powerful emotions brought about by a life change as significant as the one you're experiencing might be more than you can handle single-handedly. There's really no reason you need to label some emotions as those you "should keep to yourself" and other emotions as those you "should share." That's just another form of judging your emotions, as futile as trying to sort them out and label them "good" or "bad," "right" or "wrong," "better" or "worse." Using a trusted friend or loved one who listens well—without judging—can give you the perspective or altitude you need to move from the mindset of "right/wrong" to a mindset of "it works/it doesn't work."

The Vision

I t's very easy to get caught up in the minutiae of life. Just think about what we all have to deal with every day. We have our households to maintain. We have cleaning up to do—morning, noon, and night. People need to be fed, and that means shopping and cooking and thinking about what the next meals are going to be. There are jobs we have to do, bills that must be paid, accounts kept, repairs made. There are people we want to stay in touch with, and that means birthdays and social plans and emails and phone calls and letter writing. Then all the family matters—and the minutiae multiply furiously if you have children who need to be schooled and cared for, picked up and dropped off, clothed and fed and comforted and coached and directed and entertained.

All those things—the minutiae I've just mentioned—are merely the tip of the iceberg if you are also in a wheelchair or dealing with a medical condition or chronic illness placing constant demands on your time, energy, and attention. Now, in addition to other daily obligations, you also need to pay attention to medications and therapy, arrangements for home care or assistance. Transportation is a constant challenge. Access is a frequent problem. Depending on how restricted you are and what care you need, your daily activities may require a great deal of time, especially if something goes wrong or someone fails to show up. There are sure to be days when just getting through the minutiae seems, in itself, a monumental accomplishment. And you wonder: *how can I think about, feel, or do anything more?*

Of course, there is any number of ways you can add on a layer of expectations for yourself. You can probably come up with a list of things—either in your own mind or on paper—that you would like to accomplish by the end of the week. Then you'll break down the list into daily task or goals, and then cross them off, one by one, as you make your way through the week. If all goes well, you will succeed in ticking things off your list, meet your artificial deadline (the end of the week), and have the satisfaction of saying, "There—I finished everything." If not…well, begin next week's list with things you have not yet accomplished and see whether you can succeed.

A good plan—intellectually. Decent advice—probably. But isn't there something missing?

A while ago, I participated in a workshop where the teacher asked each one of us to come up with a personal "Statement of Desire." Initially, I thought, "Well, this will be the easiest thing in the world to do." I have so many desires, every minute of the day, where do I begin? I certainly hate being in a wheelchair, I get frustrated and enraged about all the things I can't do, and it's no picnic having multiple sclerosis. So…when someone asks me what I desire, *where do I begin?* Don't I want to be able to get out of bed in the morning, take a quick shower, and go manage my creative design business? Yes! And I want to run on the beach and swim in the sea. I'd also like to get up and down stairs by myself, and to stroll around art exhibitions—not to mention being able to get in and out of a restaurant without rearranging all the chairs, get on and off a plane without all the wheelchair hassle, and hop on a train any time I want to get to Center City Philadelphia.

But then, as I looked more closely at this "assignment" and began to understand what it really meant, I realized that a "Statement of Desire" was quite different from all these impossible fantasies and wishes and longings. The question was not, "What do you dream about?" or "How do you change who you are?" The question was "What do *you* desire?" And, given that question, I had to think about the real me—the *me* in a wheelchair, the *me* with MS, and also the *me* who had a real desire to do something with the life that I have been given. I wasn't being asked to create a "Statement of Wishes" or a "Statement of Escapist Fantasies." Statements like that would just feed my frustration and anger about the person I *couldn't* be and all the things I *couldn't* have. But a statement of *desire?* That would focus on what I could have, could be, could do. Yes, I thought, I should be able to come up with that.

Then something very interesting began to happen. As I worked on that statement, I realized the process was becoming less and less mental, and more spiritual. The "desire" moved farther away from making lists and accomplishing tasks. It became something bigger, more encompassing and over-arching. The desire came from some place very deep within me. It was bigger than any single intention. Before I even knew what my desire *was,* I realized I already knew how it *felt.* It was like a blanket wrapped around me, not suffocating or stifling but comforting and reassuring—a blanket that I carried with me when I got up in the morning and pulled up to my chin before I fell asleep at night.

Above all, this over-arching purpose, this desire, was something that transcended the minutiae. Knowing my desire—feeling it deeply, internally, spiritually—I did not really have to worry about how long it took me to get through the morning routine. It didn't matter that I am a person in a wheelchair or a person with MS. I could easily make lists of things to do and add to that list, and leave it unfinished (no matter how much you do, there will always be more to do), without counting up my daily accomplishment-of-chores and measuring my "achievements" in those terms. A vision or mission to drive me forward, put all the minutiae in context, and transcend the limitations of my physical body—that was my *desire.*

What It's Like Being You

I magine stumbling upon the Garden of Eden in an abandoned warehouse. That's what it was like for me entering the Philadelphia Flower Show.

It was March 1991, and outside, the skies were gray, the trees leafless. The bite of winter was still in the air. In the Civic Center, the world was transformed into a haven of outrageously flamboyant color. And the fragrance! It was almost overwhelming—a fantasy landscape where every flower, every vine, every leaf was enjoying the fullness of a conjured springtime.

I vividly recall my scooter, too. It was clunky and huge (not at all like the one I have today—which is a fashionable, sleek, metallic-green model), but I could steer it and maneuver it with very little assistance. Which meant it was good enough for me. Some months before, I'd taken this scooter on a very significant "trial run" on Peace Prayer Day, a "day of prayer for world peace" event I attended at the U.N. General Assembly Hall in New York City.

It was at this event that I realized, for the first time, that people were not staring at me. They did not pay any attention at all to my scooter. What they saw instead was a woman of courage, inner strength, and dignity. My spirits soared! I participated in the U.N. event with a feeling of complete freedom, as if the machine that toted me around did not even exist. And now, here, at the Flower Show, I was hoping that once again I would be able to enjoy the feeling of utter liberation that I had experienced once before.

So much in life seems to change—*does* change—when anyone, man or woman, aging adult or handicapped child, becomes wheelchair bound. That designation in itself, "wheelchair bound," speaks volumes. The wheelchair binds us. It becomes our sole means of transport, the wheels we rely on for motion, the position from which we see the world. Even though the wheelchair provides mobility, we immediately begin to think of ourselves as held back by its limitations.

That, at least, had been my first experience of life in a wheelchair. I had raged against its confinement, cursed the illness that forced me onto its wheels. I had regarded the wheelchair as an enemy. It had affected not only my self-perception but all my relationships. People stared at it, or tried hard *not* to stare at it—yet transmitted, with their averted glances, the pain of embarrassment and the fear of contagion-by-association. I had felt as if they would never be able to see my identity apart from my wheelchair.

Everywhere I went, it seemed, my wheelchair presented as many problems as it solved. It couldn't climb stairs. It couldn't get through doorways that "normal" people could stride through without a second thought. My wheelchair needed ramps, electric doors, the constant attention of a friend, a family member, a caregiver, my husband Michael, or the spontaneous assistance of kind strangers. I was part of my wheelchair, and my wheelchair part of me. It had become a constant reminder of entrapment, of my differentness.

And yet...

Something very important had happened when I attended the U.N. event in that clunky scooter. It seemingly disappeared from under me. Yes, I was still the same seated figure moving through a crowd in a motor-powered vehicle. Yes, all my physical limitations were just as they had been previously. But my mind, my soul, and my feelings became liberated. I was free, and totally caught up in the experience of joining in a cause I believed in, as an equal among all those who surrounded me.

Now, as Michael and I rode the elevator down to the floor of the

Flower Show, I wondered whether I could have that feeling again. In the years before I was diagnosed with multiple sclerosis, I had always excitedly anticipated the Flower Show. I loved the thrilling profusion of blossoms and the palette of infinite colors that greeted the visitor descending from a March landscape of beiges and grays. But that experience was in the past, before the diagnosis, before the wheelchair, before I had allowed my identity to change from "normal" to "handicapped." Could I reclaim the sense of freedom I had felt in the years before the beginning of life in a wheelchair— the freedom I had tasted once again, so briefly, at that U.N. occasion? Would I be able to forget the machine that allowed my movements and, instead, let my heart, my soul, and my imagination be absorbed by the visions of springtime that would surround me at the flower show? Could I just be *Linda* and not *Linda-in-a-wheelchair*?

And yes, it did happen! I forgot about my scooter. It wasn't part of me. I forgot about my illness. It wasn't me, either. I was simply *there*, relishing the present moment.

After this pivotal realization, I found my whole world beginning to open up. I could easily plan outings to concerts or museums, or even to the mall. I began to travel—to New York City, Sarasota, Florida, the steep hills and inclines of San Francisco, and eventually to Israel and Egypt. And I made discoveries that, I believe, apply to anyone who is wheelchair bound.

As difficult as it is to let your guard down and take a look at what's going on inside your heart, I can give you this reassurance:

> *There are a variety of strategies you can use to help you through it, and to make it far less frightening and painful than you might expect.*

> *I'm not saying it's easy to look fear in the eye, or let the rage course through your body, or*

feel that place inside where your heart is broken.

But with a good plan in place, and some good techniques you can use again and again, you can do it. I promise you that, in the end, you'll find it's a lot easier than waging a life-long battle of trying to keep your emotions at bay.

Best of all you'll open your heart to the peace and happiness that emotional freedom has to offer—and that you so richly deserve.

The Secret of the Inner Voice

From the time when we were little children, we have been trained to look outside ourselves for answers—to our parents and in the world around us. We can train ourselves to look within. This inner strength often is reached only in times of crisis. Then we realize that we can, of ourselves, do nothing except turn over our problems to a higher power. As long as we are trying to find solutions with our own strength, determination, and intelligence, we are not successful on a permanent basis.

So we repeat our mistakes over and over in new ways.

Finding our inner strength is quite simple in terms of how to do it, but it "seems" to take great effort to do it constantly. To find our inner strength, we must first listen to our inner voice. And to reach our inner voice, we must give up our attempts to solve problems with our own conscious, intellectual, busy minds. We need to give up the belief that we know what has to be done. We must be open to all possibilities, and we must resort to the strength and wisdom deep within us.

The process of inner listening is not mystical, magical, or even difficult; although to the uninitiated, it may seem that way. There is tremendous spiritual power within us. It gives us strength, vision, success, and peace. We all use this power to some degree—and no one can totally lose it, but few realize its full potential. This power is reached in a most unusual way by "going inside" ourselves. Many have searched for it in countless ways, but few have found it because it is hidden where most never look, "inside."

There are three steps to finding your inner voice:

The first step is to realize that we cannot solve or even identify our problems with our "worldly mind"—the conscious mind that we often identify as being us.

Second, we must know that we have the power within us to solve our problems, and that we can strengthen this belief to the point where we are willing to let go of all our worldly efforts to find a solution and be guided only by our "inner voice." This "listening" may take the form of sensing, paying attention, or intuition ... and having little to do with listening from our physical ears. Notice repetitious signs and your inner guidance, as this can yield valuable information. Anytime you hear something three or four times, especially within a short amount of time, it's information worthy of your attention.

And thirdly, we must have the courage to take the final step: Do it.

We must calm our conscious mind of all its busy worry, all its attempts to find the solution, and go deep within us—beyond the noise—to the quiet and peace that is always within us. For example, this can take the form of meditation, and we can use all types of tools such as being in a quiet place, assuming certain bodily positions, or utilizing special items like incense and candles.

But these forms and tools are not really necessary. We need to reach the calm and peace within us, giving up our conscious efforts, only for an instant. A trained mind can do this in any situation in the blink of an eye, and our minds become trained by our willingness to turn inside on every possible occasion.

We recognize that we are successful when we feel a sense of peace and power coming over us. We are now in contact with our inner guide. We begin to realize that we are taken care of in all things, and that we will be told if and when actions are necessary.

Our purpose for attaining this sense of peace is not to be told to do something, but to realize that we are safe, cared for, and at peace. We are in touch with our spiritual strength—the power of all creation, the order of all things—the principal that governs in peace and harmony.

When we know this, a problem no longer exists. We realize that the "problem" is not a problem, and that we can proceed in strength, confidence, and peace. If something needs to be done by us, our inner voice will tell us what to do. If we need something, the universe will send it to us. Now we can proceed calmly. We need not hurry, search, or change things. We can step back and be guided and cared for.

If I were given the opportunity to present a gift to the next generation,
it would be the ability for each individual to laugh at himself.
-- Charles M. Schultz

The False Self and the True Self

S ocrates said, "Know thyself." In Shakespeare's *Hamlet*, Polonius cautions, "To thine own self be true." But what self are we getting to know? To what self should we be true? Where is the self located anyway? On second thought, which self is reading these words?

These questions pondered by playwrights, philosophers, and other serious thinkers—if answers could be worked out through mathematical calculations, mathematicians and scientists would be the most enlightened people on planet. But the self continues to elude the greatest thinkers of our age.

What I know is, there seem to be two voices.

The first voice—the *false self*—judges and criticizes: "I'm not good/rich/thin/smart enough," or "Now that I'm in a wheelchair,

I have to prove myself," or "I am now unlovable."

Our humanity comprises only a small part of the rich experience available to us as total beings. As human beings, we all put a great deal of effort into trying to be who we think we are supposed to be; this is the *false self.*

The false self is also called the personality or ego. Some aspects of it are inherited; others are developed through experimentation with families, friends, and the culture we live in—our education and our religious upbringing. Though aspects of the personality may change over a lifetime, the false self tends to become frozen and rigid, full of regret and resentment over missed opportunities.

The need to control is probably the most prominent characteristic of the false self.

It is from here that many characteristics spring, because the need to control often runs our lives. This is ironic, considering that we have so little control over reality and what happens in the world around us. The need to control inevitably leads to frustration and disappointment.

The false self's characteristic need to control sends it on a search for power from external sources. We have to seek outside ourselves for something that makes us feel good.

We are constantly looking for that event, that nod of approval, that recognition that will make us feel more secure. This constant search for approval is evidence of the false self's insatiable need for recognition by any means, even negative ones.

Even when the false self is able to break out of a rut, it usually jumps into another one. A new marriage may repeat the patterns that doomed the previous ones. Giving up smoking often leads to overeating.

What are some of the aspects of the false self?
The false self...

- *Needs to be right, make others wrong*
- *Needs to control and dominate; runs life*

- *Searches for power from external sources*
- *Seeks outside ourselves for something that makes us feel good*
- *Has an insatiable need for approval and constant recognition*
- *Has a tendency to judge self/others, makes irrational comparisons*
- *Is full of regret, disappointment and resentment over missed opportunities*
- *Tends to become frozen and rigid*

What are some negative beliefs and/or feelings of the false self?

- *Being in a wheelchair, I am powerless, helpless and invisible*
- *I can't do it myself*
- *I'm all alone*
- *I have lost my sensuality*
- *Others do not want the burden of being my friend*

As stated earlier, the false self functions in the realm of personality and the ego. In this realm, we identify with what we look like, what we do for a living, how much money we have. The false self is like a spoiled, jealous child—always wanting to be number one.

It wants you to believe that you are your body.

Contrary to what your false self will let you believe, you are perfect the way you are. Rather than feeling inadequate when you see that someone else has more worldly or physical success than you, ask yourself why you can't accept yourself the way you are.

Ask yourself what would happen if you shifted your perspective? Instead of seeing yourself as a stressed out human being grasping for enlightenment, for some kind of spiritual experience, think of yourself—as Pierre Teilhard de Chardin so eloquently put it—"as a spiritual being having a human experience."

Is there a way out? Yes, but not through the false self. When we live in the false self, our lives are narrow, confined, and repetitious. Another notable characteristic of the false self is its tendency to judge. Judging others feels good in the short term, at least. It gives us a momentary sense of superiority and strength over those we are judging.

We also use judgment to put ourselves down. We may spend an unnecessary amount of time comparing ourselves to others, and when we find that they have things we don't have, we beat ourselves up. We may tell ourselves we need to improve, which sounds very well intentioned, but is really a subtle form of self-judgment.

The true self—the second voice—is our true guide, supporting and acknowledging: "I am healthy, resilient, intuitive and courageous." The true self affirms our true essence, which is love.

The true self encourages you to use your wisdom. Intuitively, you know not to abuse your body, or corrupt it by taking into it things that would disturb or destroy the natural nerve functions. You know to take into the body those things that will make it healthy, those things that will give it strength and beauty. This is exercising wisdom. Wisdom is given to all but few choose to use it. If you choose to use your wisdom, you will get many chances to do so.

Wisdom goes beyond the distance you travel in life or the facts you accumulate along the way. Wisdom is the responsible use of knowledge and experience. If you're wise, you keep learning all your life. Wisdom is a beginning, not an end. If you're wise, your door is always open to new knowledge, new experiences, new roads to travel. Wisdom has no boundaries or fences. If you're wise, you're not afraid of new ideas, because you know that you can always decide to accept or reject them.

You will discover the source of your wisdom. Some people think wisdom is found in the encyclopedia, the dictionary, universities or libraries (or in the online versions of these!). It may be in other books, too, or in your little son or daughter. But you will probably find that wisdom is within you, because wisdom comes from Spirit, and Spirit is within.

The Journey of Awakening

Quick cures are very appealing. Life today is so busy and complex that we will do anything to solve our problems as quickly as possible. But I see it differently. Life is not a problem to be solved; it is a journey of awakening, and that journey is not a race. *You can run, walk, or crawl to enlightenment . . . the pace is up to you.* But trying to change the false self by judging it is a method doomed to fail, because judgment itself is a product of the false self. You'd simply be going around in circles.

As Einstein pointed out, "You can't solve a problem with the same consciousness that caused it." The false self seduces us into thinking it can cleanse itself of negativity.

We may judge ourselves for overeating or overspending and then get angry with ourselves in the name of purging our perceived inadequacies. Yet we continue to overeat and overspend. This is the human dilemma—even when we want to break an attachment to self defeating behaviors, we don't. We merely exchange one false self pattern for another.

The path to control is a *futile one*, inevitably leading to frustration and disappointment. *One thing that we always need to remember is that the false self is just an act.* Whatever we do in the false self—worrying, being impatient, judging—is merely a performance.

Life is a journey of awakening, and that journey is not a race.

We don't have to change anything. But we may want to change our perspective, our outlook on life.

Things to act upon and questions to ponder:

- *How do you hold yourself back?*
- *Recall a time when you have done this.*
- *What beliefs and thoughts are you holding that limit you?*
- *What mistake are you afraid of making?*
- *What mistake have you made that you have not let go of?*
- *When you hold yourself back, in which part of your body do you feel tightness or imbalance?*
- *What needs to be loved right now?*
- *Place your hand over your heart and feel the loving going in and through your body.*
- *Forgive yourself for any judgments you are holding against yourself.*
- *Describe how you're feeling inside.*
- *What have you learned?*

Unconditional Loving

erhaps the best way to move out of the false self and into the
true self is to use the most powerful tool at our disposal—
unconditional loving.

In other words, don't let anything you do—no matter how
wrong, petty, shameful, or scary—get in the way of your loving. Let
your loving embrace every part of you, because that loving and that
joyfulness that comes with it is truly who you are.

Unconditional acceptance is the way to deal with the false self,
so that we may live in our spiritual nature.

Please pause for a minute to read this poem to yourself silently.
Then read it aloud. And listen:

I love myself even though I feel uptight
I love myself even when I am pretending to be something I am
not
I love myself even at those times when I'm feeling anxious
I love myself even though I am judging
I love myself when I am comparing myself
I love myself when I worry
I love myself even when I am being egotistical

So what exactly is the true self? Think of a person who seems
to radiate something special. What is that quality? As children most
of us had someone in our lives—a relative perhaps, or a neighbor,
or a teacher, or a local shopkeeper—who always had a smile for us

29

and a twinkle in their eye. Without knowing why, we were drawn to that person. He or she may have had a hard time, a difficult life, but somehow managed to avoid judgment, bitterness, and cynicism; and managed to transcend the human condition. In other words, that person *lives from the center we call the soul or the true self.*

Take a few moments and think about that person.

What are some of the aspects of the true self?

- *Loving or the action of love*
- *Integrity*
- *Cooperation*
- *Spiritual practice*
- *Joyfulness*
- *Enthusiasm*
- *Fulfillment*
- *Acceptance*
- *Peace*

My spiritual teacher, John-Roger, poses a question: If we are indeed spiritual beings, then why—when the false self is running around screaming and beating us up—doesn't the true self do something to stop it?

Answer: Perhaps the true self is waiting for us to be quiet and pay attention to it for a few minutes so that it can impart its wisdom and love. To connect with the true self, we need to leave behind the behaviors of the false self and emulate the behaviors of the true self.

Another way to attune yourself to the true self, is to give full attention to the rising and falling of your breath. Observe your breath in a neutral and loving way. By simply observing the breath, we begin to move further into the field of the true self. And as we do, we feel more joyful, more enthusiastic, and more naturally loving about the human experience, no matter how crazy it seems at times.

Practice Living in the Moment

When practicing "living in the moment," you release outdated negative thoughts, feelings, and beliefs; and recognize lifelong patterns that no longer support you. With "new eyes," you begin to recognize and celebrate the extraordinary human being within you.

You come away feeling lighter, more loving, more forgiving, and more grateful, for having had the courage to move on with your life. You can let go of the past and create an inspiring future.

It is possible that much of the difficulty we experience in life, and much of the joy we miss, is the result of being who we're not. It is possible to be who we truly are, to enjoy the harmony and balance of being aligned with our soul.

Caught in Rush Hour

It was rush hour on a humid day in August in Philadelphia and my husband, Michael and I were stuck in traffic on the way to a doctor's appointment. He was complaining: "This ride is taking too long! It's so hot in this car! We're gonna be late! That idiot in front of us doesn't know where he's going! Now he's on his phone! What a *!% #*!!!"

I was hot and tired, too, because the air conditioning in the car was not working properly. Sitting next to him, I chose to direct myself to be peaceful in the present moment—not to resist anything—and accept the situation *as it was*, instead of commiserating with him, agreeing and joining him in his moaning and whining *(even though, believe me, I didn't like it one bit either)*.

What were my choices here? We couldn't control the number of cars on the road or improve the driving ability of the people behind the wheels, or change the hot, humid Philadelphia weather for that matter! We couldn't alter the circumstances, but I had a choice in the way I related to the situation. *After all, how you relate to the issue is the issue.* So I sighed, and turned to Michael, and said gently, "Honey, you might as well put on some soothing classical music. Let's open the windows—don't you love the delicate scent of foliage in an oncoming storm?" (It looked like we were about to get a summer thunderstorm!) "And let's say a silent prayer for that guy in the car ahead of us; he may be confused and not be consciously aware of where he's going; he might even be lost."

Accepting the moment resulted in the sweet peace that was the present moment. This recognition was all it took for Michael to return back to himself. It startled him when he realized that he'd spent the last ten minutes annoyed and resisting the way it was. He smiled at me, and thanked me for bringing him back to himself. Certainly, his behavior was not consistent with who he is. And by the way, we did get to our appointment on time, calmly and in peace.

I exist as I am, that is enough,
If no other in the world be aware I sit in content,
And if each and all be aware I sit in content.
One world is aware and by far the largest to me
*   and that is myself,*
And whether I come to my own today or in ten
*   thousand or ten million years,*
I can cheerfully take it now, or with equal
*   cheerfulness, I can wait.*
--"A Song of Myself," *Leaves of Grass* by Walt Whitman

Part Two
Awakening Your Spirit

The sole purpose of a man's existence
is to kindle a light in the darkness of mere being.
-- Carl Jung

The Road Map:

Life Lessons to Awaken Your Spirit

The Road Map is my name for whatever it is, in you, that provides guidance in navigating the path to the Soul. The spiritual "laws" that we will explore in subsequent chapters are the foundation of the map. Each law is a kind of marker along the road. When you can apply even one of these laws, you are on the right track to living from the true self.

It is your challenge and your responsibility to attune yourself to the true self within, so that you may find wisdom. Wisdom is using those things that work for you for as long as they work for you, and letting go of the things that are not working for you. Problems are beautiful, because every time you handle or overcome a problem, your wisdom and your knowledge grow, which means that *you* grow. Overcoming your problems gives you strength to go further. Your circumstances are your stepping stones. They give you an opportunity to learn and an opportunity to gain wisdom.

The four basic spiritual laws are ACCEPTANCE, COOPERATION, UNDERSTANDING, and ENTHUSIASM. Each can be applied to any situation to bring you back to your center and into alignment with your true self. We will supplement these four pillars with the additional building blocks of CALM/STILLNESS, FORGIVENESS, CREATIVITY, CREATIVE THINKING, COURAGE, CONNECTION, GIVING BACK, FREEDOM, GRATITUDE, and TRANSFORMATION.

With the four spiritual laws as your foundational guide, you can take any issue, situation, or challenge—relationships, health, finances, career—and move from a false self view of it to the true self perspective. For most laws/pillars, you will find an exercise in the book's Appendix where you will be able to apply this "false-self-to-true-self" method to a particular issue or situation that you are facing.

In the midst of movement and chaos, keep stillness inside of you.
-- Deepak Chopra

Calm/Stillness:

I Am Centered in Truth and Peace

C alm/stillness is the sacred space within you. Once you are in touch with it, you become very relaxed and peaceful, yet dynamically aware. The more you inhabit this space, the less inclined you will be to give up the space to judgments, fears, or negative beliefs and habits.

When we are still, and accept *what is,* we are more able to make sound decisions and judgments. This is an essential cornerstone to a lifetime of powerful behavior that ultimately will lead to manifesting infinite possibilities. I believe that calm and stillness are the most important markers because they serve as a foundation for the remaining steps.

Calm is the universal state of fulfillment, the result produced by being present in the moment. It is a result of the interaction between what you think, feel, say, and do.

Discovering the Calm/Stillness

I came of age as part of the Woodstock generation and the Age of Aquarius, seeking a new way of life and looking for fulfillment and meaning. At age 19, I was thumbing through a book on Buddhism, entitled *Be Here Now* (Ram Das, 1973). Reading this book would forever change the way I thought about life. It showed me how to begin to find freedom and peace daily within myself. This book pointed out how to use negative or difficult situations as a path to freedom and enlightenment. It demonstrated ways to let go of suffering, which is caused by holding on to attachments, desires, and wants. For me, a valuable interpretation of Ram Das's message was to find the flow of life and follow it—*not resist it.*

I was not fully aware of how this profound classic would blaze a new spiritual trail that would shape and awaken not only my own consciousness, but the consciousness of a new generation. This book taught me *to strive to be fully present in my life, and maintain that focus..*

When you resist life, there is something for negativity to latch on to. But if you just accept it and let it flow, it will go right past you. If you resist life, you get stuck. This "find the flow, and follow it" is a lesson I have never forgotten. It is not always easy, but it is fulfilling when I achieve it! It was a relief to me, and began to form the context for how I have lived my life from that point forward, up to the present.

When you see others, look into their hearts, not to analyze them,
but to find where you can touch them with your love.

-- John-Roger, *Divine Essence*

Acceptance:
I Accept All Parts of Myself

A cceptance is the ability to let go of our perceptions of how we believe things should be (or shouldn't have been), to relax, and to let in the reality of what is.

Acceptance is one of the most important principles in the awakening into spiritual awareness. Acceptance asks you to accept any situation as it is and to accept yourself as you are. You accept what is. The law of acceptance is actually very logical: when you set aside your feelings and thoughts and negative fantasies, all that's going on is *what is*.

- Acceptance is a point of view—your outlook on life and your frame of mind.
- Acceptance is giving up control, not suffering, and embracing the moment.

- Acceptance opens up possibility. As a result of our choosing to accept our reality, the opportunity to experience peace can occur.
- Accepting things as they are is a choice. When we have a more positive and accepting focus, we can choose how to respond to (or relate to) each of our circumstances.
- It doesn't mean that we don't whine, struggle, or bang our heads against the wall when things don't go our way.
- We have aches and pains. We get older. We lose independence.
- *This is the point where we choose to accept things as they are.*
- Then we can get on with our lives and move forward.

Acceptance doesn't mean we agree with, like, or condone what is going on. We may think of ourselves as open minded and objective, but in fact our approach to ourselves, our circumstances, and other people, is often obscured by pre-existing notions and ideas—which are influenced by our values, our past experiences, our upbringing, and events around us.

The law of acceptance allows us to look at every situation as a stepping stone on the path to awaken our Spirit, and use every situation as our teacher.

As human beings, we make mistakes. However, inner growth often comes through making mistakes, but many people cannot make a mistake without self judgment. Acceptance offers another choice— instead of beating yourself up for your mistakes, you can accept them! We all have heard that we can seldom control what happens in life, but it is always in our power to choose our response.

I Am Not My Body

After a physical therapy appointment, on a sunny day in June, 2007, my homecare nurse wheeled me backwards down a ramp that led to the exit door and to the parking lot. Neither one of us noticed the damaged and uneven pavement and the slight crevice between the ramp and the platform leading to the parking lot. The back wheels of my chair caught on the lip at the lower edge of the ramp, thrusting me forward, and catapulting me out of the chair onto the asphalt. I landed flat on my face.

I remember the second I felt the wheelchair on the lip. The next moments were in slow motion. I felt as if I had left my body. I saw myself fall out of the chair, and then lying on the ground.

I could have judged my aide and yelled at her angrily. I could have reported her to her supervising agency. Or, I could have consoled her, hugged her, and acknowledged to her that it was an accident. I chose the latter, which meant not struggling with the way it is. I fell, I didn't get hurt, it was an accident, and that was the story. Everything else was drama. I chose to be calm and peaceful. I asked my aide if she was all right.

I knew instinctively that there was nothing wrong and that I was okay. All around me people were running up and shouting, "Oh my God, are you alright?" And I calmly said, "Yes, I'm fine." I was scared that I might have injured my bones because of osteoporosis, but I was peaceful and calm. The ambulance came. The two hunky attendants lifted me—I didn't fight it. One of the attendants, Tim, talked eagerly about his life. And since I'm a minister, I listened. His fiancée, their trouble in selecting a wedding date, and deciding where to live. By the time I got to the hospital, I knew his whole life story, and told him I would keep him and his fiancée in my prayers.

When I saw my aide again inside the hospital, she was crying uncontrollably. I hugged her again and consoled her. I told her that I was shaken but all right. I was concerned that I might have torn something in my right shoulder and arm. After seven hours and 26 X-rays of my head, neck, shoulders, chest, and back—and a CAT scan—it was an absolute blessing that I came away only with a limp, a temporarily paralyzed right shoulder, arm and hand. I was hopeful that the damage was minimal. To my knowledge, nothing was broken (and especially not my spirit!).

The lessons I came away with that day were tremendous. My Spirit is much stronger than my body. I am NOT my body.

A Day at the Beach

I have always loved the beach—taking long walks, splashing at the ocean's edge, running and jumping in the waves. As my legs got weaker, there became no way to be on the beach without being carried. Several attempts at rolling a conventional wheelchair onto the sand for beach experiences resulted in sinking wheels and tears of frustration and longing to be where I so loved to be.

One summer I heard of a new type of all-terrain wheelchair that was designed specifically to bring people in wheelchairs closer to life outdoors. Michael and I searched and ultimately tracked down this chair, and it has been a miracle for me. With its large pneumatic tires, it rolls easily over sand, gravel, grass and other outdoor surfaces. In 2003, for the first time in nearly twenty years, I experienced the freedom of dangling my feet in the ocean while sandpipers, egrets, pelicans and hundreds of other sea birds and creatures surrounded me. My heart (and my toes!) experienced freedom and possibility because of that fat-tired wheelchair.

Another miraculous experience Michael and I had with a manual wheelchair was the opportunity to tour Egypt, visiting the pyramids and other ancient sites, touring museums, and exploring all the stops along the Nile River, from Aswan to Luxor. We have also been to Israel, where we experienced the history and tradition of my Jewish upbringing and the energy of the Jewish homeland, walking all over Jerusalem and again experiencing the ocean's edge.

Freedom results when we make uplifting choices. This why the Emily Dickinson quote, *"I dwell in possibility"* has always meant so much to me.

When you're losing sleep, reviewing and worrying about a problem, it usually means you're not *accepting your situation*. Similarly, when you're upset with yourself, it generally means you aren't self-accepting. When you are judging yourself, you have strayed off the path to accepting yourself. This is the moment to reach for this guidebook.

Look at your life right now. Look at the choices you exercise.
Are they all in support of health, wealth, and happiness?
Are they all in support of unconditional loving and no judgment?
If they're not, you are not yet cooperating with the opportunities of
your divine plan.
-- John-Roger, *Passage Into Spirit*

Cooperation:

I Flow with Life; I Let Go of Always Being "In Control"

Once you accept a situation, the next step that awakens your spirit through adversity is Cooperation, another marker on the journey. Unconditional cooperation with whatever is happening is one of the keys to creating happiness and well-being. It is a powerful antidote to stress.

Cooperation has a lot to do with letting go. When we cooperate, not only do we let go of the need to be better than others, which reinforces the False Self and ego, but we also let go of our resistance to change and to not getting our way. Once we have accepted the reality of *what is*, we can go with the flow. We stop trying to control

42

other people or bend situations to our will. To get the idea of what this means, picture a surfer riding a wave. He's not trying to push the breakers or hold back the tides but to become so attuned to the movement of the water that he and the wave are one.

Thinking about cooperation, I vividly recall an experience where I became conscious of my true self. There is a wonderful Chinese proverb: "Don't push the river; it flows by itself." This is to remind us of how much of our lives we spend "swimming against the current"—and getting nowhere—only to discover that our true success and inner peace are found when we respect the river and go with the current.

Down the Rapids

Many years ago, Michael and I went on a white water rafting trip on the Cheet River in West Virginia. I wanted to prove to myself that even with multiple sclerosis I could be courageous and daring, doing whatever I wanted to do. We came to an area in the river appropriately named Killer Rapids. Crashing through the churning waters, the boat bucked and heaved, violently thrown this way and that by the tremendous power of the river.

Suddenly, I was thrown from the safety of the boat into the rushing waters, hitting my head on a rock and breaking my nose. The force of the river pulled me under, and a part of me just let go, *cooperating,* flowing with the river, not resisting it.

I have never known such peace. I heard choral music sung by a melodic choir; I smelled the sweet fragrance of tropical flowers; I saw flashes of purple and white light; I heard a clear voice saying, "Do not fear; you are safe. I will always be with you."

At that moment, I remember making a promise to myself, that no matter what, I would find this peaceful place again, this inner place of loving. It was a place of total cooperation, accepting what was in front of me, flowing with the water, not resisting, and not fearing what at the moment seemed like imminent death.

So many times, when I find myself playing the victim and fighting my illness, I try to remind myself of that white water experience.

You may moan that life is unfair, that you don't deserve the bad things that happen to you. Perhaps you would like to have more money, a more creative job, greater health, greater happiness, or closer relationships. How might you be blocking the kind of cooperation that would bring those to you?

Attitude is one big factor. When you are in a state of cooperation, your attitude is one of joy. If you are asked to do something, you do it—and then some. You not only do the job at hand fully and completely, but you might also look ahead to the next project.

Because you are cooperative, your focus extends beyond your immediate needs and desires. You are always thinking, "What else can I do for you that will assist you even more?" A side benefit of being cooperative is that your creativity can come to the fore. For example, Michael asks me if I want the door closed because I'm feeling chilly. But he not only closes the door, he also checks the windows for drafts, turns up the heat, and offers me a sweater or anything else he can think of to make me more comfortable. This "willingness to go the extra mile" describes true cooperation.

Serious illness is like the Cheet river in my story. It can come at us with a relentless power that can fill us with fear and despair. But if we can find the perfect place of peace, we can cooperate, flowing with the current and surrender to its power rather than fighting it.

As you use observation and compassion to discover opportunities for cooperation, you will experience a profound sense of freedom. Cooperation empowers us and allows us to look beyond being victims of circumstance or slaves to our own illnesses.

"How shall I help the world?"
"By understanding it," said the Master.
"And how shall I understand it?"
"By turning away from it."
"How then shall I serve humanity?"
"By understanding yourself."

-- Anthony de Mello, *One Minute Wisdom*

Understanding:
I Let Go of What People Think; I Am Good Enough

The next step that awakens your Spirit through adversity is Understanding. After we *accept what is* and *cooperate* with it, understanding appears. It is not a mental or intellectual process, rather it means *being centered,* resting in the peace and calm of the unconditional True Self, where there is no measure of 'greater than' or 'less than' anyone or anything else. This type of understanding brings balance, calm, peace and tranquility.

In order to find this understanding, we need to see past what we think *should be* and move on to *what is.* This means seeing the world without negative judgment, even when the False Self is endlessly parroting its needs. It means seeing past our conditioning, which can distort reality to conform to the positions we take. The true source of our inner and outer conflicts (and thus not being able to find understanding) is our failure to realize that we are spiritual beings, and that understanding must come from within.

If you are unable to stay in the present moment, life can seem overwhelming. The best way to confront any new challenge / circumstance is to take them one at a time. With each new challenge, take a few moments to become still, and then move into being patient (with everything, including yourself). You may have to be patient for a day, a month, a year while simply observing the situation. If you maintain a sense of patient and loving observation, you will be able to outlast the difficulty and better understand it.

You can deal with *any* challenge in this way: lovingly extend your spiritual energy field and encompass the situation, then maintain neutral observation. This approach places you securely in your center. Then, from this center, spiritual energy starts radiating outward. It does not radiate as personality, but as an expression of your spirit.

A few things to keep in mind as you continue the journey toward understanding:

- Self-absorption kills understanding and compassion.
- Judging ourselves and others is automatic and habitual, so it is important to be conscious of this response.
- Judgment can appear to be "justified" by something we or another person have done or have failed to do.
- Judgments limit and cripple us, and can lead to us being unable to forgive ourselves or others.
- Understanding or compassion is not pity, worry, or feeling sorry for someone.

- We equate worry with love, but worrying does not show ourselves or others love. It takes us out of the present moment and empowers the false self and its negativity.

Forgiveness is the only way to true health and happiness.
By not judging, we release the past and let go of our fears of the future.
In so doing, we come to see that everyone is our teacher
and that every circumstance is an opportunity
for growth in happiness, peace and love.
-- Gerald G. Jampolsky, M.D.

Forgiveness:

I Forgive Everyone, Including Myself

Trrue forgiveness is unconditional, and includes forgiving ourselves. To forgive is to be willing to let go of any hurt, guilt, or resentment that we feel in regard to another person— or ourselves. If we are holding on to a perception of self-blame, for example, emotionally beating ourselves up because of something we did or failed to do that we feel might have prevented the illness we have today, that perception accomplishes only one thing: it causes us stress.

Most people think of the term *forgiveness* as accepting an apology or letting go of an old grievance for a past harm another person has done to you. We "forgive" a debt or we "forgive" a loved one who has said something hurtful. However, there is another meaning of forgiveness. It means letting go of your past perceptions.

Similarly, if another person was in some way responsible for our present illness or physical condition, we may be "holding a grudge." It is not unusual for one who has been seriously injured by another person's negligence to say, "I will never forgive her!" What we don't realize is that clinging to this past perception causes us pain and stress. *And clinging to it can never harm anyone but us.* The fact that we did something or someone else did something is of little concern. The real problem begins for us when we judge what happened as wrong, bad, mean, hurtful, nasty, improper, and so on.

We hold so much against ourselves and against others; then we hold it against ourselves that we hold things against ourselves and others. The process of judging ourselves and others for not measuring up to our perceptions is a painful one. For this, forgiveness may be the greatest healer.

It's our judgment *against ourselves* we really need to forgive. The action was just the action. Our judgment that the action was bad, mean, and so forth, is what caused our stress. This is not the same as denying that the harmful situation happened or saying that it really doesn't matter. Certainly it matters!

And surely you would do everything possible to avoid putting yourself in the position of getting injured again. But when we cling to blame or take the stance that we will "never forgive" the person who we feel is responsible for our pain, we are literally creating part of the "dis-ease" we wish to heal. Self-forgiveness is a promise to yourself that you will not cause yourself any further pain by clinging to these perceptions, thinking that by doing so you were punishing the other person (or yourself). Our lack of forgiveness in such situations is, in fact, part of the disease—and we can heal it. We do this by recognizing that blame (and self-blame) is a specific kind of perception that we can let go of, thus freeing ourselves from its painful grasp.

Forgiveness always needs to begin with self-forgiveness.

Sometimes, when people learn that they have a serious illness, they begin judging themselves for not seeking medical help sooner, before the disease had progressed to the present stage. Again, it is *your judgment* that the action was wrong—the action itself is not the issue, at this point.

The process of forgiveness does not require the participation of anyone else. The process is a simple one:

To forgive yourself, begin by saying the following out loud to yourself:

- "I forgive myself for not seeing a doctor sooner." (To me, this means I will forgive myself for anything I did or did not do in the past. Instead, I will be responsive to life in the present as I remember who I am.)
- "I forgive myself for holding on to those perceptions that cause me pain." (To me, this means I will release myself from negative perceptions.)
- "I forgive my parents [or others] for being emotionally repressive." (To me, this means "I will let go of any blame I feel toward my parent. Who I am today is my responsibility."

Any of the fears or other negative self-judgments you may have uncovered in this chapter are opportunities for you to practice forgiveness. Forgive yourself for judging, knowing it was the judgment—not the action—that caused the pain, hurt, and separation. Remember, you are not saying that it does not matter that you or another person did something to cause your present pain. But that was then, and this is now. Unhook yourself from the past so that you can be at peace with your life today.

Self-forgiveness is an inner process. When we start to wonder, "Who am I?" it's time to turn to the silence within. In that silence, we listen. Whenever you feel that you are out of touch with your loving, simply move into the quiet center within. The way to your loving is through the true self, which is unconditional and unconditionally loving.

Remember this key point from the earlier chapters: The true self doesn't need fame or recognition or approval, but the false self is like a celebrity who needs a lot of attention and who screams and shouts until he gets it.

True enthusiasm comes from participating with God's energy.
When you're attuned to Spirit, this energy is unwavering.
But unless you continually reconnect with the source, the spiritual
energy within you will dissipate and eventually disappear.
Therefore, it's essential to take time for yourself.
Time alone, in silence, allows your true self to reawaken and
reconnect with the Divine.
Then Spirit can flow through your body, mind, and emotions,
generating enthusiasm on which you can ride.
-- John-Roger

Enthusiasm:
I Rise Above All Limitations; I Let Go of Productivity as Self Worth

The next step to awaken your Spirit through adversity is Enthusiasm, a first cousin of positive expectations. Enthusiasm comes from the Greek word, *entheos*, "having the god within." When we go deep inside—past our thoughts, emotions, and doubts—we can tap into this spiritual energy and utilize it to improve our lives. We can also share it with others, which can result in a tangible contribution to improving the world around us.

Enthusiasm gives us the ability to stay focused and achieve what needs to be done with surprising ease, accomplishing things we never thought possible. We so often rely on caffeine or adrenaline for an energy boost, or pushing ourselves way past midnight to meet a deadline, but soon enough the effect wears off, leaving us exhausted. True enthusiasm is the natural way to energy that's long lasting.

True enthusiasm comes from participating with your Higher Power's energy. When you are attuned to Spirit, this energy is unwavering and does not wane. But unless you continually connect with the source, the spiritual energy that is within you will dissipate and eventually disappear, leaving you again exhausted and drained. This is why it is essential to take time for yourself. Time alone, in silence, allows your true self to reawaken and reconnect with your higher self. Then Spirit can flow through your body, mind, and emotions, generating the enthusiasm you seek.

In time, you'll learn to reconnect with this energy as easily as you breathe in and out.

Breathing in awareness and breathing out enthusiasm becomes as regular as your heartbeat. As you make a habit of continually reconnecting to you Higher Power's energy, the Soul replaces the personality as the center of consciousness. The Soul will use the body, mind, and emotions as the vehicles through which it expresses and functions in the world; but instead of being distracted by your personality, you will be living in the clarity of the Soul, and free to experience enthusiasm; and ultimately, joy.

Joy often seems scarce, especially for women, who are often displaced by stress and the perceived obligation to take care of everyone else. I remained too long disconnected from what brings me joy. I tapped back into the joy; I fondly remembered my childhood dream of becoming a prima ballerina. On the beach, I felt the breeze on my face, the sun, the wind. I joyously became the rhythm of the water. I noticed the call of the seagull and the laughter of children. I smile more and connect with new friends. For too many years, I buried my joy beneath endless tasks and deadlines . . .

I drive my electric scooter filled with joy. I am grateful for the feelings of independence, and freedom of movement. Given my circumstances, joy didn't happen overnight. I'm still learning, but these days I go to bed peaceful, not harried. I have clarity and energy. I've created a life that allows me to generate an income doing what I love.

Post-diagnosis, I felt a desperate need to clarify who I was and what I stood for. I began to measure joy within the context of disability—this definition has evolved over the years. Today, joy is being free, staying in the moment, and manifesting my love for God. When confronted with adversity, I hold to my values and principles. I no longer feel trapped by my circumstances. I feel authentic joy.

I continue to reclaim joy in my life. I remember not too long ago watching ballroom dancers practice outside my chiropractor's office. I had a bittersweet memory of a jewelry box my grandmother had given me when I was five. A tiny ballerina, in a pretty pink tutu, spun around and around as the music played. Watching the ballroom dancers, I reclaimed the joy of the gift, and of my grandmother's love.

True enthusiasm is the natural way to energy that's long lasting. Unless you continually reconnect with the source of this energy, the spiritual energy within you will dissipate and eventually disappear. Enthusiasm is a key to maintaining and, at times, rediscovering this spiritual energy.

Creativity is just connecting things.
When you ask creative people how they did something,
they feel a little guilty because they didn't really do it; they just
saw something.
It seemed obvious to them after a while.
That's because they were able to connect experiences they've had
and synthesize new things.
-- Steve Jobs

Creativity:
I Have Unlimited Potential; I Let Go of Comparison

Another marker along the roadmap that awakens your spirit through adversity is Creativity. When we allow ourselves to be creative, we take risks. Creative risk taking means daring to explore your talents, to think outside the box. To be creative is to design, change, rearrange, or even get rid of something. To create is to invent, to bring something into existence that wasn't there before. Creativity comes from tapping the passion within ourselves. The core of creativity is to be accepting, to be willing to take risks (be courageous), and to have the desire to create and reinvent a more optimistic way of living. We can create a way of being for ourselves that currently might be unrecognizable to us as really being us. Creativity and reinvention go hand in hand.

Many years ago, I read of a woman in California who has Parkinson's disease. She continues her work as a psychotherapist, thanks to having her office in her home. In her spare time she has planted one of the most beautiful flower gardens I have ever seen. Living in California, she has included many exotic plants, such as orchids and bird-of-paradise. Her garden has become a place of healing not only for her but for her clients, and even strangers who pause at her fence to enjoy her artistry.

I think of Auguste Renoir who, because of crippling arthritis, reached a point where he could no longer hold a paintbrush to paint. He began strapping brushes to his hands and painting with longer, more fluid strokes to create some of his best works. Henri Matisse was confined to bed in his later life and was unable to work with paints. Instead, he created huge, stunning compositions from colored papers that he cut out with scissors as he lay in bed. Van Gogh, Toulouse Lautrec, Gauguin; these artists were masters of reinvention. They used their will and passion to transform the creative process by expressing their art and leaving the world with their life's work, regardless of their mental or physical disability and suffering.

These artists were my teachers and role models of transformation. I love to paint with watercolors and created pieces prolifically. Years ago, I sold out three one-woman shows in order to pay for the tuition needed for my first husband to attend Jefferson University Medical School in Philadelphia.

Later, as illness affected the mobility of my hands, a new symptom surfaced: a tremor in my painting hand.

There was never a question that I had to find another way to express my lifelong passion. Instead of trying to prevent my right hand from trembling, I had a jolt of inspiration and began to USE the trembling to create rhythmic strokes of color and movement, resulting in tender and sweet art that reminded me of beautiful

Japanese calligraphic paintings. Today, forty years later and still right-hand dominant, I have accepted my mostly paralyzed right hand as it lies motionless on my lap. Even when typing these words, I muster all my energy, focus, resilience, passion, determination, and heart, and carefully hunt and peck on the keyboard with my index finger on my left hand. On some days, I "write" by audio taping my thoughts, and have my assistant transcribe the text for me.

Expressing myself creatively has always been my calling and the gift I have been given. In order to honor this passion to create, there has been a seismic shift in the perception of my creative life: an exercise in "letting go of the form." Be flexible, and give up any attachment to the way things were in the past and what I could physically do then. I stay in the present moment, relax, and trust that creativity will show up in perfect timing. I am grateful to the role models before me who set the standard of excellence by creating, no matter what.

Discovery consists of looking at the same thing as everyone else
and thinking something different.
-- Albert Szent-Gyorgyi, 1893-1996; Nobel prize winner

Creative Thinking:
I Am Not Afraid to Break the Rules if it Would Lead to New Ideas

I t has always fascinated me that creativity and positive thinking are often born out of limitation. When there is adversity, it seems, we humans have all the greater incentive to work out ingenious ways to overcome obstacles, protect ourselves from harm, and chart new territory. I've recently encountered someone who embodies that spirit of creativity overcoming adversity, Kevin McGuire, a wheelchair user who created AbleRoad.

Of course, we've had to do this since the beginning of human history. We've always been vulnerable, and there was a time long ago when we were ill equipped to defend ourselves from bears, wolves, and saber-toothed tigers. But we used our creative minds to survive. And we continue to do so. Now, with so many mechanical and human aids at our command, we have unheard-of opportunities that would have been unimaginable to our ancestors.

So I ask you, "What makes a creative person tick?" A creative person wants to know about all kinds of things—ancient history, Impressionist paintings, the works of Plato or Rumi or Eckhart Tolle or Springsteen, flower arranging, the lyrics of an Elton John song, current food manufacturing techniques, Turner Movie Classics, accessibility issues, (or lack of access to people with disabilities), the impact of technology, and the future of healthcare—never knowing when these ideas might come together to form a new idea. It may happen six minutes later or six months or six years down the road. True creativity has no timeline.

It just may be that any limitation, in itself, is a springboard into creativity and abundance, just as our physical bodies are the springboard into the Spirit.

Before the onset of Multiple Sclerosis, I had a flourishing career as an artist. While that career was necessarily cut short, my love of art remained undiminished. But how could I practice my art? My right-hand tremor made it impossible to hold a paintbrush steady. There was nothing I could do, or change, that would allow me to paint the way I had before.

But I didn't give up. I was reminded me of Auguste Renoir who, because of crippling arthritis, strapped brushes to his hands. He had to paint with longer, more fluid strokes, but painting that way resulted in some of his best works. I also remembered Henri Matisse, who was confined to bed in his later life. Unable to work with paints any longer, instead he created huge, stunning compositions from colored papers that he cut out with scissors as he lay in bed.

As I thought about what I might do, how I could once again practice the art that I loved so much, the solutions of these artists made me think that what seemed impossible might in fact be possible. These artists, in fact, became my teachers, role models of the highest forms of creative thinking and transformation. Their example reminded me that I needed to change my attitude. Instead of dwelling on what I could no longer do, I had to explore the possible. It required a change in attitude, or outlook, which inspired me to explore how I could still paint! It was then I had a jolt of inspiration. Instead of trying to prevent my right hand from trembling, I began to *use* the trembling to create rhythmic strokes of color and movement, resulting in tender and sweet images that reminded me of beautiful Japanese calligraphic paintings.

The creative mind really does have the power to transform one thing into another. But too often, we become fraught with anxiety about our limitations. By changing perspectives, and playing with our knowledge and experience, we can make the ordinary extraordinary and the unusual commonplace.

The creative person, I've found, holds on to the faith that it will happen. Knowledge is the stuff from which new ideas are made. But knowledge alone won't make a person creative. I think we've all known people who knew lots of stuff but were unable to apply their knowledge in new ways. The real key to being creative lies in what you do with your knowledge. Creative thinking requires an attitude or outlook which allows you to search for ideas and manipulate your knowledge and experience.

Fortunately, there are unlimited examples of creative humans who applied their knowledge and ingenuity to the world around them. Johann Gutenberg, the creator of a printing press that utilized movable type, combined two previously unconnected items—the wine press and the coin punch—to create an unprecedented invention that would make printed books available to millions of people. The purpose of the coin punch was to leave an image on a small area such as a gold coin. The function of a wine press was to apply force over a large area in order to squeeze the juice out of grapes. Gutenberg asked himself, "What if I took a bunch of these coin punches and put them under the force of the wine press so that they left their images on paper?" The result was an invention that radically changed the history of civilization.

Today, the rewards of creative inventions are spilling over into every aspect of our lives. I could name scores of extraordinary thinkers, artists, and inventors who have made life easier for us all— and, particularly for those with physical or mental limitations. Those creative people have opened doors for us both literally and figuratively. As I move about my house, answer messages, make calls, travel, read, and write, I am incredibly thankful to the remarkable individuals who dreamed of doors that would open automatically, computers that would respond to voice commands, motors that would propel wheelchairs, and the numerous other devices that would have been impossible to imagine even a few decades ago.

And the breakthroughs continue. To name just one example of a person who has followed this life-changing creative thinking expansion, I think of Kevin McGuire who has been instrumental in the creation of AbleRoad. Kevin was inspired by his work with Paul Allen, co-founder of Microsoft. AbleRoad is developing breakthrough technology and a website to assist people with disabilities (PWD). With AbleRoad people using wheelchairs—as well as those with medical issues or mobility, hearing, vision or cognitive disabilities—can review any public space in their world. Once a space has been reviewed, AbleRoad makes this information available, letting others read reviews posted by people who have a similar disability and making it easy to research and choose the businesses they want to patronize. Visitors can also use the AbleRoad's smartphone apps to submit their ratings: http://www.ableroad.com

People with Disabilities, as well as their families and caregivers, can remotely view restaurants, stores, hotels, concert venues, and other public places that are rated for factors like wheelchair accessibility (also ease of access for blind, low vision or deaf people). AbleRoad has the potential to change the world in so many ways. McGuire has made it his mission to see that public venues around the country -- and eventually worldwide -- are accessible to everyone.

Where will all this lead? For anyone who faces any kind of adversity, creative thinking cannot make all the obstacles go away. Even the most ingenious solutions cannot change the reality of what we live with. But the very process of finding new solutions, discovering novel ways to put together the familiar to create the impossible—in the tradition of Johann Gutenberg, Kevin McGuire, and so many others—is sheer inspiration for us all.

So, here's a question for you to ponder: What do *you* have in common with other creative thinkers? How do we open ourselves to expand our thinking?

Maybe what it takes is a closer look at what seems impossible. Figuring out a new way to hold a paintbrush. Or how to combine the capabilities of a wine press and a coin punch. Or how to use the power of the internet to peer into public places and see whether it's safe to venture there.

The next time we feel that we don't have enough money, or we can't have what we want, we can see it as an opportunity for creativity. Instead of being disempowered by what we are faced with, we can see what is possible, and begin there to realize what can only be imagined. That's how we can all use the power of limits to expand our reality.

EXERCISE:

1. **When was the last time you came up with a creative idea?**

       ------ **This morning**
       ------ **Yesterday**
       ------ **Last week**
       ------ **Last month**
       ------ **Last year**

2. **What was it?**

3. **What motivates you to be creative?**

We delight in the beauty of the butterfly,
but rarely admit the changes it has gone through
to achieve that beauty.
-- Maya Angelou

Courage:

I Am Strong by Embracing Vulnerability

An important step to awakening your spirit through adversity is Courage. The original meaning of courage is from the Latin word *cor* meaning "heart"—so the root of the definition means share all of yourself, share your whole story, with your whole heart. An act of courage is an act of storytelling. Courage means that you try your best even when circumstances are scary or difficult, and/or even when your success isn't guaranteed. This is the first thing we need to understand about courage. What I've learned about aging through illness is that courage means facing the things that I've been afraid of, whether real or imagined—the monsters of what I imagine might happen to me, the monsters of the future.

It takes courage to embark on a new experience or adventure—

for instance, to relocate to a different region of the country (or world), or to make a new friend, or start a new business. It takes courage to break a bad habit or take a stand to make a difference in the world. And it takes courage to reinvent ourselves by looking at how we could spend the rest of our lives, or the next week or the next month or even just today. And you and I know it takes courage to strip away everything that we think we are and reveal what and who we authentically are.

***

A Perceptual Shift

My mother has suffered from Parkinson's disease for a number of years, which causes tremors of the hands, arms, legs, jaw and face; rigidity/stiffness of the limbs and trunk; slowness of movement; and impaired balance and coordination. This progressive disease usually leaves a person incapable of initiating and controlling movements in a normal way. Compounding this is the fact that she has recently been diagnosed with cancer of the bone marrow, which devastated her and left her seriously depressed. These diseases have not only robbed her physically, but have also robbed her of the desire to participate in any activities other than going to the dining hall for meals.

Michael and I went for a Sunday visit with my mother when she was at the Abramson Center for Jewish Life, a nursing home/assisted living community about 30 minutes from my suburban Philadelphia home. There was a concert going on in the town hall, a community gathering area at the facility. There must have been 100 people there of varying physical and mental ability. There was a violinist, accompanied by a piano player, performing delightful music that the residents seemed to be thoroughly enjoying.

My mother was a classical pianist before she was married to my father, and I knew she would revel in the concert. Not seeing her there, I went to her room and found her sleeping, just like she does on most afternoons. Michael and I gently roused her and enthusiastically told her about the concert that was going on downstairs, hoping to convince her to go. Of course, she did not want to go. She resisted us with statements about how much trouble it was to get dressed, fix her hair, put her makeup on, etc.

Michael and I insisted that she go because we knew she would love it. We requested an aide to help her get dressed and ready to go downstairs. By the time she was dressed, in her wheelchair, and down the elevator and into the town hall, the concert was over.

I saw her disappointed face and decided to act. I went over to the violinist who was packing up to go. I asked him, "Please—I know that this is a bold move, but would you take a few more minutes to play something special for my mom? It took time for her to get dressed and come down to see you, and she was too late and missed the whole concert. It would really lift her spirits if you could play something, given that she made the tremendous effort to dress and come down here to hear you play."

Without skipping a beat, he consented and gave her a private concert for about 10 or 15 minutes. The few people who were left in the room gathered around and joined us in experiencing this little private concert. When the violinist finished, Michael approached my mother and said, "Rita, now it's time for you to sit down at the piano and play." Now, my mother had not played the piano for four years, not since my niece Dani's bat mitzvah, for which she practiced daily on a portable keyboard. Since then, the keyboard has gathered dust in her room; so of course, she flatly refused to play. "No I can't do that. I can't do what I used to do. I know I'll be disappointed in myself. I'm tired; my fingers hurt and my hands are stiff; and I should go back upstairs and rest." We persisted, "But you used to love to play!" Ignoring her protests, Michael wheeled her over to the piano.

I watched her face and saw the thoughts racing through her mind. She was conflicted—"I'm not doing this. I don't think I can. I don't remember anything." Then suddenly, at a moment when I was turned away for a second (in the blink of an eye!), I turned back to see her tentatively lift up her hands and begin to play with stiff fingers. As she played, she lost herself in the music, and for a brief moment in time, did not judge herself. She played expressively, Michael at her side encouraging her. I was so overwhelmed that tears began to roll down my face. Residents were stopping to watch and listen to her playing. People were even taking photos! It was extraordinary to witness her transformation.

I told her how inspirational it was to see how courageously she played, despite her negative and judgmental thoughts. I exuberantly (and tearfully) expressed how monumental it was to hear her play again. I enthusiastically suggested to her that she should play every week, saying that it would give her something to look forward to and alleviate her boredom.

She immediately said, "Oh, I couldn't! I can't do this like I used to." My response was, "Mom, I can't do what I used to do either. I now type with one finger, and my fingers don't work either. I can't even straighten them out. To me, it's a big deal that you just played the piano like you did for ten minutes or so. That's inspirational for me! Thanks for being a courageous role model for me."

This is the first that I remember being a witness to an actual perceptual shift. My mother didn't think she could play the piano, but she did. She tapped something inside herself that shifted her perception of herself from fearful to courageous. It was as simple as that. And it happened in the blink of an eye.

**

You can deal with any challenge in this way: lovingly extend your energy field and encompass the situation, then maintain neutral observation. This approach places you securely in your center, your Soul. Then, from this center, spiritual energy starts radiating outward. It does not radiate as personality, but as an expression of your Soul's light.

There are two ways of spreading light—to be the candle,
or the mirror that reflects it.
-- Edith Wharton

Connection:

I Am Connected to All of Life

The definition of connection is knowing another and being known by another. In her groundbreaking book, *Daring Greatly*, Brene Brown says, "Connection is the energy that is created between people when they feel seen, heard, and valued; when they can give and receive without judgment." As our lives get busier and we cram more activities and appointments into our schedules, and increase our pace of accomplishment from a jog to a trot to a sprint, it becomes an out-of-control spiral of do, do, do. Most of us feel disconnected not only from our partners and loved ones, but also from ourselves. Creating authentic intimacy and connection with those we love means putting aside our electronic gadgets, our schedules, and our to-do lists, and opening our ears and hearts and exploring what it takes to simply listen to each other.

Connection and intimacy are interwoven and dependent. They

are symbiotic—one cannot exist without the other. Intimacy is having nothing to fear and nothing to hide. It is rare, and precious. It requires honesty and kindness, trust and forgiveness. Intimacy is being seen and known as the person you truly are.

We can take action, doing something to heal or soothe ourselves and others. You might wonder "Is it enough that my objective is to spend quality time with my family?" Yes, of course! Once again, it is not the magnitude or number of people you affect that counts. What's important is the engagement of the heart.

One man I know likes to do jigsaw puzzles with his grandchildren. Paralyzed following a stroke, he and three of his grandchildren get together at least twice a week to do puzzles together; but the real reason he does this becomes obvious only when you see them together. Beyond the puzzles, there is a communion of hearts that literally lights up the room.

***

The Fear of Connecting

One spring, I hosted a table at the National Multiple Sclerosis Society fundraising luncheon in Philadelphia: Women Against MS. It was unsettling for me to notice that I couldn't get through my lunch or maneuver my scooter among the crowd without seeing someone reaching for a cell phone or *already talking or texting on one.* The unfortunate message sent out to the people present may be "there is someone else I'd rather be interacting with than you."

I wondered to whom the people at my table could be speaking with on their cell phones between the appetizer and the fish entrée. You would think that we all could have found someone in the room to relate to, given that we were all there for the same reason—ridding this world of Multiple Sclerosis—instead of being distracted by our smart phones (and temporarily removed from the event). The thought occurred to me that maybe most of us *fear intimacy and deep connection* even when we are sitting next to each other at a fundraising luncheon supporting a cause that we all have in common.

Our days are filled with beeps and pings, many of which pull us away from tasks at hand or face-to-face conversations. We may feel that the distractions are too much, but we *can't* seem to stop posting, texting or surfing. The benefits are obvious: checking messages on the road, staying in touch with friends and family, efficiently using time spent waiting around.

Even while we're standing next to each other... we choose technology to communicate. From texting at dinner to posting on Facebook from work, or checking email while driving, on a date, or sitting across from each other at a restaurant, the connectivity revolution is creating a lot of divided attention, *not to mention social angst and separation*—ironically the very opposite of connection!

When someone starts texting at a party, or at a business meeting, or at a luncheon, it may be taken as an *insult* by those physically present. The downside is that we're often effectively disconnecting from those in the same room. Psychologists agree this is not good and it's time we take a good look at what we are creating. *We've come to confuse continual connectivity with making real connection.* We're always 'on' and available to everyone in our social and professional circles at every minute; and they are available to us.

When you actually look more closely, in some ways we've lost the time for the conversations that count. Listen closely, everyone, I want to remind you that technology *can* be turned off.

***

It's no surprise that, with to-do lists a mile long and overloaded and multitasked schedules, most of us *aren't even aware that intimacy and connection are missing from our lives.*

We may even feel lonely, and not know why. Something feels "off." With each new gadget or next new thing we acquire, we learn how to connect with others in a new way. We teach our brains how to deal, reorder, repackage, rethink and reinvent. We are getting smarter and faster, yet more and more isolated. We can no longer assume we have someone's full attention when we're physically with them. We're saying to each other in one way or another that *we can always put each other on "pause."*

As we go through the aging process and experience grief and loss as friends and family pass on, the need for connection to extended family, friends, community, and to all of humanity, becomes even more important. *Being connective means being ready to connect.* In other words, each time we connect with someone, we should treat the experience with awe and respect, as if it were the same offering of Spirit, not unlike the handwritten letters of yesteryear. We should realize and be grateful for all the things that matter—beauty, love, creativity, joy, inner peace—*and begin to awaken to what really matters to us ... and why.*

***

The Power of Connection

For the past 25 years, most of my waking hours have been spent in a wheelchair. Of course, all my family and intimate friends are used to seeing me this way, and we've all had plenty of time to adjust to the challenges I face anytime I want to go anywhere, much less try something new. But I always wondered ... what will it be like for people who knew me in my younger, wheelchair-less days—when I was an optimistic, energetic teenager hanging out with my friends, doing all the crazy things we did together—to see me as I am today?

I was born in 1949 and raised in Philadelphia, the City of Brotherly Love, which was already becoming known for the soulful, sensual "Sound of Philadelphia"—that Philly sound that embodied the era of rock and roll in America in the '60s and '70s. In the early 1960s, the hugely popular *American Bandstand* show with Dick Clark, which originated in Philadelphia, was a massive influence on my friends and me, and the rest of the teenage record-buying public of the country.

The '60s was a fun and a unique environment. Just talk to any baby boomer who was a teenager during the '60s and they will tell you how fun it was and how fortunate they were to grow up in the 1960s. School dances and the dance crazes during that time were something else.

Growing up in that environment, I loved to dance! In Philly, where most new dances were shown first on *Soul Train*, I observed carefully, imitated and learned my first dance steps by practicing for hours in front of a full-length mirror. My high school girlfriend Joyce was also an avid learner, and once we had mastered the dance steps of the Mashed Potato, the Bristol Stomp, the Pony, or any of the other complicated, coordinated line-dance steps that appeared so easy on television, we set out to teach all our other high school girlfriends. We squealed with laughter and joy every time we were on the dance floor. Looking back, those seem like infinite, boundless, never-ending, joyous days. I danced for freedom of expression, and I danced for my life.

All that was years before multiple sclerosis became my teacher and lover, and my bright green wheelchair became my permanent dance partner. What is, is what is supposed to be, or it would not be. The rest is up to us. But, I have learned somewhere along the way that I just had to learn to trust life (and to trust God).

So when I received an invitation to my 45th high school reunion for the Class of 1967 from Northeast High School, I seriously wondered what this experience would be like. Many if not all of my classmates probably knew about my MS. In many ways, I knew, our relationships would be just as strong as before. I looked forward to seeing the whole gang and hanging with my old friends Jake, Steve, Marty, Stan, Bruce B., Shelly, Lisa B., Sherry, Eddie M., Louis, Karen, Lynne, Joyce, Fred, Bobby, Chuck, Helene, Howie, Stuart, and Skippy (who will always be Harry to me). I knew that we could talk and laugh about the good times and lasting friendships we shared.

All that I anticipated with relish as I eagerly accepted the invitation and began looking forward to this upcoming reunion. But what would I do when all these dear friends began to dance, as I knew they would? How would I feel then? I closed my eyes and sat quietly, aware of the rhythm of my breath.

It happened in April. As I entered the Radisson Hotel in my

electric wheelchair, the air was filled with the soulful music of the '60s and '70s—Smokey Robinson and The Miracles, Gladys Knight and the Pips, The Temptations, Martha and the Vandellas, The Four Tops, Stevie Wonder, Donna Summer. I was instantly swept back in time to 1967, and my mind was flooded with the memorable times and defining moments that I experienced with my classmates back then.

My friend Joel was the first one to grab me on the way in. "Hi!" he shouted. "Do you remember me?" I replied, "Of course, I do, Joel! You're still as handsome as ever!"

After that, it was all greeting and kissing and hugging. Essentially, we all looked the same as we did 45 years ago. (Well, sure, most of us are grayer. Some men are balder and some have bigger bellies, but of course the girls looked fabulous!) I loved how naturally the girls and guys teased and flirted with each other, just like they did back in the day. I did not see them as they are now. I saw each of them as my lifelong friends from high school, four-and-a-half decades ago in our world. As I individually connected to the light behind their eyes, the teenagers I knew so many years ago smiled knowingly back at me. I experienced the warmth of our human connection as we are all brothers and sisters. That love and connection we had, and still have, comforted me.

And then something extraordinary happened. Even though I'm in a wheelchair, people grabbed my hands, shouting enthusiastically, "Dance with me!"

Dance? Me? They meant it.

My wheelchair was not a factor. All my friends, these exultant partygoers, seemed blinded to its very existence.

That night, I never left the wheelchair while I was dancing, but my spirit was free from it. I was not ashamed, embarrassed, or self-conscious—only free and exuberant and joyful. I was totally in the moment.

***

Living with MS, a progressive illness, has forced me to accept sudden changes in life that are not always easy or pleasant to deal with. Accepting and loving myself—overcoming fear, embarrassment, and self-consciousness—was a significant milestone for me. I can honestly say it turned out that probably 95 percent of the things I was afraid of, I had no reason to be afraid of. Every day I am still working on that: dropping my fear and just ... letting it go.

I realized I had not only given myself another opportunity to dance again, I had also given that chance to my classmates to see me, and be with me, just as I am today. We shared a wonderful past and were totally caught up in a splendid present.

At that moment, I was happy. Right there and then. Not the next day, not 10 minutes from then, not after the reunion was over, but right there and then, in that moment.

It was a magical night!

As you realize your life is a gift, move into your gratitude.
Find your natural willingness to give from the overflow
that is your abundance and prosperity.
Look for ways to honor your relationship with God.
-- Unknown

Giving Back:

Now Is the Only Time There Is; I Let Go of Scarcity

Another step in the road map that awakens your spirit through adversity is Giving Back. When you truly give to others, you don't expect to receive anything in return for what you have given. You give with a free and open heart and without keeping score. Real giving is unconditional. We can learn, or re-learn, unconditional giving, be it with money, wisdom, time, creativity, or by sharing a practical skill or life experience. Keep these ideas in mind the next time you have the opportunity to help someone; you may be helping yourself as well.

For example, 70-year-old Lois Swartz and her husband, Cy,

have been politically involved since they were young adults. They are actively involved in "Bubbes and Zaydes (grandparents) for Peace in the Middle East," a peace and justice group that works to end the illegal occupation of the West Bank territories of Israel. My late Aunt Lottie Plaut, at age 93, created quilts that she donated to terminally ill children. She organized a group of quilters to make and send five hundred quilts to the hurricane Katrina victims. Lottie said her life had always been about connecting with and helping people.

Giving can also define who we are as individuals. I believe that who we are is what we give because in the end, we are what we have given. We talk about giving time and attention, of giving hope, love, of giving a break and giving money. The most important part of what we give is not necessarily the check we write, but the transformation in the life of the recipient of the check. In this act of generosity, we may recognize that real caring is unconditional, no strings attached. When we are truly acting generously, we don't stop and think about whether the recipient deserves what we are giving. And in the long run, we may attract love and respect from others because we have given unconditionally.

Tony Castellano, age 90, was a former middle weight champion and department store detective who kept the gate at a secured Florida retirement community and cheerfully gave out grapefruits and oranges to all who passed. Tony believed that "all people were put on the earth for a good purpose and that doing harm to anyone will cause an imbalance." He also says, "I have survived breast and colon cancer, and feel that I am living a form of a charmed life. I love people."

Lan Yin Tsai is an 89-year old Asian bicyclist I met in 2003 at the 150-mile National Multiple Sclerosis Society bike ride. She told me about the unconditional commitment she has to the MS cause upon completion of her 18th annual ride, this one in a persistent, cold September rain. For Lan Yin, service and charity define her commitment. I was at the finish line in 2003 when a Philadelphia newspaper photographer took photos of this 79-year old woman in a skirt and high heels, perched on a three-speed bicycle, a treasured gift from her sister in China. Lan Yin's story is a great example of reinvention and a living demonstration of the message that inspiration to give beyond one's own needs and desires is a key tenet of knowing what your life is about. "I try to do my best every day in whatever I do," says Lan Yin, "knowing I shall be remembered for how I have lived each day. I wish to give not only to my family, but also to as many people as I can."

My cousin Mel Barton, 90, has always been an inspiration to me. We have had a special bond since I was a young girl. A World War II veteran, Mel earned a Doctor of Podiatric Medicine (DPM) degree and enjoyed a 40-year career in his profession. He remains active in several professional groups, and also volunteers for many organizations, including as an usher for the local theater. He is truly an inspiration to all who cross his path, including his three grown daughters and three grandchildren. His advice: "Be true to yourself, be honest, treat your family as if they are the most important people in the world, study hard to attain your goals, honor your friendships, give to your community, be conscientious about your health habits, and take care of yourself. Finally, no matter what – keep going."

Libby Keenan, age 67 and a recovering alcoholic with many decades of sobriety, spends time in nursing homes reading to, playing games with, and just talking with older people. "People over 90 are my biggest passion because, as I am getting older, I am realizing that older people become more invisible to the world. You have to be involved with other people. You have to give more than you think you are taking. The thing that puts a smile on my face is the one day every week that I spend at the nursing home. I have programs that I am now doing. If [these people] die feeling that the rest of the world saw them as invisible, they are going to know that at least one person cared about them—me."

I met Burton Young, age 75, for the first time when I attended a performance by the New Horizons Senior Center Glee Club. Burton was the master of ceremonies. "I entertain two, three, four times a week at senior residences, clubs, and nursing homes and bring my show (standard songs, jokes, singalongs, and oldtime vaudeville skits). If my life were to be ending soon, I would hope to have a performance at some nursing home on the way to the cemetery!" I loved his spirit and enthusiasm!

Most of us don't discover our life mission in a few hours or even a few days, though there are certainly stories of people suddenly getting a vision of their mission through a dream or in a flash of insight. For most of us, however, a clear picture of our mission comes about only through the effort of looking very closely at our lives and following the wisdom of our hearts.

Everything can be taken from a man but one thing:
the last of the human freedoms—to choose one's attitude
in any given set of circumstances, to choose one's own way.
-- Viktor E. Frankl, *Man's Search for Meaning*

Freedom:

I Am Looking at the Same Thing as Everyone Else and Thinking Something Different

What all of us really desire, I believe, is freedom. Before we begin this chapter, I want to be clear about what I mean by freedom. Ironic though it seems, I turn to a woman in a wheelchair and a group of prisoners serving life sentences to remind me of the real meaning of that word.

The woman in the wheelchair was Joni Eareckson Tada, who had a diving accident in 1967 at age seventeen that left her quadriplegic. In 1994, Joni, working from her home in Agoura Hills, California, embarked on a mission to recover damaged wheelchairs, refurbish them, and then send them to handicapped people in other countries who were in desperate need but without any means of buying their own wheelchairs. Joni called the program "Wheels for the World." As she worked with an extensive network of volunteers in her faith-based group, Joni's vision caught on. The program grew by leaps and bounds, and after the first eleven years of its existence, Wheels for the World had more than 550 volunteers throughout the United States and had shipped more than 27,000 refurbished wheelchairs to nations around the world.

But the mission, and the vision, did not end there. "Joni and Friends" (as she calls her group) got in touch with a number of prison wardens. Would it be possible, they wondered, to set up a program where some of the prisoners could help out with the wheelchair rehabilitation program? Many prisons already had active workshop programs, employing skilled and unskilled inmates who worked regular hours for small stipends. Why not teach some volunteers the skills needed to disassemble, repair, and rebuild the chairs that were shipped to them by Wheels for the World?

A number of wardens liked the idea. Among those who decided to cooperate in the program was Warden Burl Cain, head of the high security Louisiana State Penitentiary at Angola, Louisiana. By 2005, twelve prisoners at Angola had voluntarily joined the program. At 7:00 a.m. each day, they took their places at workshop tables inside a state owned, renovated metal building surrounded by coils of barbed wire. With wrenches and screwdrivers they took apart the damaged wheelchairs, lubricated bearings, replaced broken parts, and reassembled them. Their "incentive wages" ranged from four cents to twenty cents an hour.

To Ellen B. Meacham, a reporter from *The Baton Rouge Advocate* who visited these prisoners and interviewed them, it was clear that their real incentive was far more than their meager pay. Their work area was surrounded by photographs of scores of grateful handicapped people who had regained mobility with wheelchairs from the program. The need was as clear as the mission. The prisoners knew who would be receiving these wheelchairs and what a difference it would make in their lives.

Tyrone Lindsay, a former death-row inmate (his sentence has been commuted to life imprisonment) spoke for many of the other prisoners when he said, *"This helps me regain my humanity."*

"Where I come from," he went on to tell Meacham, *"is somewhere that's nothing but the bottom. But now I'm on top because I'm doing something to help people....It's changed my whole outlook. I feel free when I do this."*

Many times since reading this article, I have wondered about the many paths of desire that lead to freedom. The desire of a woman in a wheelchair, paralyzed for decades, to deliver wheelchairs to handicapped people around the world. The desire of the hundreds of volunteers who contribute their time and efforts to the program. The desire of those prison wardens who understand (as Warden Cain of Angola put it), *"Criminals take, take, take. This is about giving back."* And the desire of the prisoners themselves, doing time for the most serious crimes, to wake up every morning knowing that they have a job to do, serving a mission that is greater than themselves.

This is what I mean by overcoming the "minutiae" of our lives. As a quadriplegic, Joni Earackson Tada has numerous daily challenges that must seem, at times, all-consuming. Each of the volunteers who assists Wheels for the World has, I'm sure, family obligations, household chores, financial commitments that could easily fill every moment of their waking hours. All of the prisoners who refurbish the wheelchairs will remain prisoners: none are promised a lighter sentence, or more leniency, or greater privileges. Yet all these people wake up, each morning, to a shared task and an over-arching mission that helps satisfy their desire to serve a larger purpose. They have their "to do lists," I am sure, but what they *do* each day is far more than tick off the items on that list.

Like the prisoners who enable others to be free, each of us has the power to experience the transformation that results in our own freedom.

What does freedom mean? It means *taking a stand for your life.* Freedom is an inner dialogue that gives voice and permission to speak out for what we believe and do what we believe is right, much like our nation's founding fathers.

Freedom is enjoying life's simple pleasures, such as

experiencing nature's wonders, or discovering the possibility of an all-terrain wheelchair, or "walking" in a motorized scooter down city streets, in art museums, or in shopping malls.

Freedom, like interdependence, comes in many different forms, and it is different for everyone. For almost everyone, it is a balancing act between accepting what one cannot change while striving to make the best of the current situation. For instance, look at Christopher Reeve, Franklin D. Roosevelt, Michael J. Fox, Helen Keller, and many others like them. Like the handful of young rebels who founded the United States, they stepped beyond their challenges and chose to explore, invent, and *take a stand for a better way against all odds.*

One of the greatest miracles is being thankful for what you have
right now.
There are only two ways to live your life.
One is as though nothing is a miracle.
The other is as though everything is a miracle.
-- Albert Einstein

Gratitude:

I Give Thanks Each and Every Day

Another step in the road map that awakens your spirit through adversity is Gratitude. The word "gratitude" comes from the root word *gratus* (Latin), which means pleasing. One interpretation of gratitude might be that when we are pleased with something or someone, we are grateful. If we look deeper within ourselves, we also might see that when we are feeling grateful, we are pleased with the world around us.

Gratitude reminds us to find our happiness in everything—in exceptional things, in mundane things, in good things, in so-so things, and even in terrible things. Our aches and pains, our new grandchild's first smile, our moments of doubt and fear, our upbringing, what our teachers thought of us, what our friends think of us, what the state of our retirement plan is, our illness, aging, the process of dying, a phone call from an old friend—all are part of an automatic feedback system directing us to pay attention. We can be grateful in both large and small ways. When we are feeling thankful, we can be more receptive to making a difference in our world.

When our hearts are open, forgiveness and gratitude evolve simultaneously, each supporting and nurturing the other. Rather than focusing on the "what might have been more, better, or different," why not start being grateful for what you've chosen? In these moments, we find our blessings. And because of our blessings, we are grateful for our lives.

I believe that when people approach the end of their life and know they have only a short time left to live and no time to waste, they open up their hearts more profoundly, knowing they have less, not more, time to live. When I review my life and pay attention to the ways I might have studied a second language or had grandchildren or bought that water property in Florida, or saved more consciously for my niece Dani's education or my retirement, or traveled to Japan; I stop, slow down, remember who I am, and forgive myself, awakening the depth of my compassion for myself. Forgiveness takes on a life of its own. I now have a 'bucket list' of what I want to accomplish before I pass on. Completing the book you are reading right now is item #3 on that list!

I am so grateful to my spiritual teachers and my husband, Michael, who have supported me and encouraged me to look inward—deeper and deeper, as I did my best to stay present and share this fantastic journey with you. *Michael, in all ways, you are the heart of this book.*

I am especially grateful to Michael, who unconditionally supports, believes in, and loves me after 34 years of marriage, during most of which I have had Multiple Sclerosis. I know that when I take the time to be grateful, I become more loving, forgiving and respectful. When I am most grateful, I feel connected to the world, and I can more easily look for only the good in all people and all events and leave the rest—the responsibility of fixing the broken pieces—to a higher power. It is only then that I can relax and truly cease to judge my own life.

I am also grateful for the simple action of using my thumbs, which I have always taken for granted; and which, in my present reality, I need to operate my electric scooter. I use my right thumb to accelerate my scooter (walk forward), and I use my left thumb to back up my scooter (walk backward). I am grateful for how my fingers grasp things and extend so I can type, or scratch my nose, or even put on my lipstick and mascara.

I am grateful for my body. It never ceases to amaze me that my body produces and destroys blood cells every second, and that my heart needs only one minute to pump my blood through my network of cells and tissue and back again. It's been doing this minute by minute, day by day, for over 64 years. Obviously, this is a matter of life and death for me, but I have no idea how it works; and it seems to work remarkably well in spite of my ignorance.

In January 2005, I was with my father in the last few days of his life, and I was reminded yet again that it is true that each of us has only a short time here on earth. Even though my dad was in a coma, I spoke to him. I shared with him everything that I always wanted to say —how thankful I was that he gave me the opportunity to attend art school, how I stole quarters from the top drawer of his dresser when I was little, how he always believed in me, and how he refereed the fights between my mother and me. My husband, Michael, is like my father in many ways; and for this, I am grateful.

Gratitude is ultimately the work of the heart.

I am prepared. I do not fear death. With the calm, stillness and inner peace I have in my heart, I often wonder if I will have enough time to complete my life to the point where I can say at the end, "I am fulfilled." But whether I have enough time to attain that fulfillment or not, I am grateful for my life, the people in it, and the opportunities that have been presented to me. I know that whatever comes forward is timed perfectly. I am grateful for the awareness to know that.

***

Limitless Gratitude

Although relating is inherent in human nature, it takes attention, care, and commitment; especially when tragedy or loss enters our everyday lives. My husband, Michael, is the love of my life, and we have discovered a more powerful dimension where relationships can become an occasion for creativity, vitality, intimacy, and self-expression. This is why the Emily Dickinson quote, "I dwell in possibility," has always meant so much to me.

It was 1978, and the evening session of the second day of the est training that I was attending in New York City, when I learned to look at the notion of possibility in a whole new light. During this evening session, this new view of possibility had an immediate and powerful impact on who I was, how I lived my life, and how I saw things—now, in the present. I realized I had the power to shape my actions and begin to shift the way I was being right now. That was the day I began to discover new ways of interacting that lead to new levels of happiness, satisfaction, and fulfillment in areas that are most important to me.

That evening was doubly enchanted because it was then that I first saw Michael. He stood across the crowded room in that faded dark purple sweater that I'll never forget. "The one—," I still tease him, "you remember, the one with the hole at the left elbow." My thought at that moment was, "This guy needs a good woman, and he's really handsome, and besides, he is great 'raw' material. In time, I just know I can change him." In the long run, though, it is I who has been changed by Michael.

When Michael and I were first getting to know each other, he took me to the health food store and walked me through, gently holding my hand and pointing out different items, naming them and telling me of the health benefits of eating organic meals consisting of foods like fresh vegetables, grains, and vegetarian sources of protein (beans, tofu, tempeh, seitan)—foods without preservatives or refined sugar. Before I knew Michael, I never had much interest in educating myself about food or nutrition. As a child, ridiculous as it sounds now, I actually thought that most vegetables came from aluminum cans!

Life changes fast . . . Michael and I had only been married for 17 months when I was diagnosed with Multiple Sclerosis. It was 1981, and I actually believed that I had the rest of my life to go dancing in high heels and red lipstick. It is said that the rites of passage are narrow, and that they come just once.

With my diagnosis, life as I knew it changed instantly. I knew that the life I had known up to this moment was slipping away. I thought about the moments that we all have wasted in our lives. They are precious, and we can never get them back.

Now, after 34 years of marriage, I am bothered when I see couples bickering. I sometimes even take the woman aside and gently advise, "Be loving now. You may not realize it, but you two just don't have enough time to waste in senseless arguments with each other. In the blink of an eye, life can change." I hope that when they see me in a wheelchair, they will think I know what I am talking about and pay more attention to what I am saying—and ideally, I hope they heed my advice.

In the late 1970s, Michael and I spent hours gyrating beneath the glittery lights of the swirling disco ball at Philadelphia's hottest discotheque, dancing to the pulsating sounds of Evelyn Champagne King, Donna Summer, and the Saturday Night Fever soundtrack. Dancing and mounds of big hair were in vogue in the seventies, and I relished every moment of it!

Since I have been in a wheelchair, dancing, walking the beach, bicycling, and other physical activities I enjoy have become bittersweet memories, but memories that I will always treasure nonetheless. We still dance, but slowly and not too often—usually at weddings and bar mitzvahs. Michael stands me up, and we close our eyes and sway to the music. I sigh. He sighs, "Do you remember when we swayed like this—my arms around you as we watched the sun set over the Sea of Galilee?" "Yes, honey," I say, my eyes glazing over with the memory, "I remember."

Other tender moments I remember with Michael: When he had me laughing hysterically in the rain as he pushed my wheelchair at the foot of the Luxor Temple in Egypt; or when we celebrated the simplicity of the morning sun rising over the mountains in Kauai; or being stunned by the purple mountain at sunset over the Badlands the time we drove cross country seeking a healing from a Lakota Sioux medicine man in the spring when the medicinal blue flowers blossom; or when we sat in silence at the Indian shrine commemorating the horror at Wounded Knee.

Sometimes the tender moments can occur during everyday activities: when we take giddy hand-in-hand walks at the mall, me riding my scooter beside him. And sometimes these moments can be sudden and unexpected. For example, we were driving on the Pennsylvania Turnpike one day when he suddenly slowed down and pulled our car over to the side of the road so he could coax a flock of wild geese and their babies to safety from one side of the road to the other. The geese were attempting to cross the road in their meandering, oblivious way, and Michael feared for their safety. I told him that was one of the most loving, romantic things I had ever seen anyone do. As dangerous as it was, it was so endearing and revealing of the kind, gentle man who was sitting next to me.

The volume of stories and memories of things I love about Michael would fill a book on its own, but here are a few that I really appreciate: He is convinced he knows how to repair a broken VCR/DVD player. He can prepare a deliciously nutritious macrobiotic meal even after I say, "Honey, there is nothing in the refrigerator." He is there when a friend or family member needs consolation because of a bruised ego, a doubting spirit, or a broken heart. He finds my hand in the dark. He loves to play devil's advocate when discussing politics as much as he loves to wear his worn-in boots or the beat up froggy slippers his sister, Shary, gave him for his 65th birthday. He is patient, easygoing, and considerate, a result of being raised by an exceptional woman—his mother, Muriel, who I was fortunate enough to have in my life for 16 years before she passed away. He opens doors for other people. He is the last to leave a conference or party because he is in the midst of conversation with a number of people. He avoids walking into a room when he senses negativity. He is still learning to trust his instincts when it comes to business and people.

Michael has a quiet, private side, too. He prefers solitude and silence. We live in the heart of busy suburbia, but we are fortunately sheltered from the noise and human activity by acres of trees and concerned and attentive neighbors whose homes are not too close to ours. There is abundant wildlife to enjoy observing and glorious seasonal changes to pay attention to—it is beautiful here and we cherish the silence. With the woods as his audience, Michael plays the piano like an angel, in the style of Keith Jarrett or Chick Correa. He also plays the flute, and has practiced yoga for the past 40 years. He is a student of martial arts and is fast becoming a master of Ving Chun.

Michael is my partner and friend—a man of genuine integrity. He is deeply honest, at times infuriatingly optimistic, and is committed to making a difference on the planet. Each year, he participates in the 150-mile bicycle ride for MS, riding in my name. He has an adventurous heart. He rarely loses his temper. In fact, the only time I ever see him become truly enraged is when he sees healthy and able-bodied people unfazed at parking in handicapped parking spaces. Their carelessness and lack of conscience make him furious!

I have had many moments of darkness and despair over the years, and Michael knows just how to distract me from my sadness. For instance, in the middle of the icy subzero Philadelphia winter, when I am complaining about being cold, Michael will suddenly tell me his favorite stupid "icy winter" joke his father probably told him when he was seven years old: "Do you know how cold it is? It's so cold that I saw a chicken with a cape on (capon)!" And I laugh every time, temporarily forgetting my discomfort and enjoying yet another reminder of why I love him so much. He knows how to lighten my heart.

Sometimes I feel like a burden to Michael. I allow myself to be frightened and vulnerable enough to wonder if he will leave me for a healthier woman, who would dance with him and walk with him on the beach, and for whom he would not have to cut food into bite size pieces. He also wouldn't have to lift her on and off the toilet at least twice in the middle of the night, or help her in and out of the car, or do any of the myriad little things he does for me 24 hours a day. But then my phone will ring and it will be Michael from some distant location where he is doing business, just calling me to say, "Hi Schmoopie!" (an endearing nickname for me he picked up from a past episode of *Seinfeld*), and to check in to see if everything is okay here at home or if there is anything I need. George Gershwin phrased it best, ". . . someone to watch over me."

Michael and I visit our local farmers market every weekend to buy fresh fish and produce. While there we have lunch at the grill (for me, a turkey burger and a cup of coffee) and visit with our friends Floyd and Betty Alderfer, who own the fish market where we buy fish. Floyd and Betty have been married for 63 years, working side by side every day, and they are still very much in love. In fact, on every day of their married life, Floyd has given Betty a fresh rose—sometimes surprising her by putting it on her pillow at night. He also makes sure that he tells her *every day*, "I love you." They are an inspiration to us, as we hope we are an inspiration to other couples, whether or not their journey is more or less challenging than ours.

I don't get red roses on my pillow at night, but several memorable occasions stand out for me as wonderful and remarkable indicators of the depth of Michael's love for me. On our 20th anniversary, in a restaurant in New York City, I found an antique diamond ring in my salad! On our 25th anniversary, by contrast, Michael gave me a little plastic organizer for Q-tips and cotton balls for my bathroom. This may not seem like much of a gift compared to a diamond ring, but I was deeply touched by this gift that met my need for order and revealed to me how well Michael knows my idiosyncrasies. He knows that I like to keep things organized, and I delighted in the thoughtfulness of the gift and the simplicity of keeping the Q-tips and cotton balls in one place.

Both strangers and those who know us well are in awe of our relationship and our deep commitment to one another, and frequently comment on how marvelous it is to have what we have. When we travel by plane, they see Michael helping me navigate a cramped airplane bathroom. When we go out for dinner, they see him helping me eat by cutting up my food and sometimes feeding me. When we socialize with friends, they see him attending to my every need, from removing my coat to getting me refreshments. Diamond rings and Q-Tip organizers aside, it takes a loving and devoted man to come home from an out of town business trip and wipe the tears from my face to comfort me after I've been sitting on the toilet for six hours, waiting for my health care aide to arrive because her car broke down in a Philadelphia ice storm.

This is love in its most real, demonstrative form.

A few years ago, I witnessed yet another example of Michael's love for me. He not only realized that two screws were missing from the steering wheel of my motorized scooter, but he stayed up half the night attempting to fix it because he knew that the following night I was counting on attending my 40th high school reunion. He will hold back my hair and wipe my forehead while I'm throwing up; or rub my shoulders when I am wracked with back pain and fear. I believe that, as we grow older or become chronically ill (or both!), these are the kinds of creative efforts and everyday gestures on which great romances are built.

It takes a real man to stay when it would be easier to leave. Because of Michael, I have managed to see myself as whole and well, regardless of what is or was happening to my body. He has taught me that joy and sorrow go hand in hand; and now, and as we both age, the marriage vow of "in sickness and in health; til death do us part" has become an integral part of who we are and who we've become.

Sometimes I wake early in the morning and find Michael looking at me lovingly. Because of that love and his commitment to my well-being, I am less alone, less isolated, and less separated from the world. He loves me, and I am still what he wants and needs. He still thinks I'm sensuous. He enjoys my feistiness, my persistence, my creativity, my resourcefulness, my silliness, and how I work and play. After all these years, we still love sharing our vision of transforming each stage of life, and with grace (and grit!), we will pass through together. Those "Schmoopie" phone calls confirm it for me. They totally fulfill me—my heart still leaps every time I hear him say it to me!

Personal transformation can and does have global effects.
As we go, so goes the world, for the world is us.
The revolution that will save the world is ultimately a personal
one.

-- Marianne Williamson

Transformation:
I Am Willing to See My Magnificence; I
Transform My Life by Being Who I Really Am

Another step in the road map that awakens your spirit through adversity is Transformation. Transformation is a metamorphosis, a shift, a transition. It is creating the next 10, 20, or even 30 or more years after you have stopped and looked at what you have or do not have, what you have done or have not done, whom you have been or not been, and what you are still becoming. Whatever your religious or spiritual approach—or even if you have no approach at all—transformation is more than change. Transformation is a process of growth, of becoming something.

As we begin to attune to that inner world, our emotions subside, our mind becomes quieter, and we find that deep within, we awaken to our Soul, our true self. We are open to receive and feel Spirit as it touches us.

We learn by direct personal discovery. Think about learning how to ride a bicycle. One moment, you couldn't ride the bike, the next minute you could. Once you have learned it, you know it forever. A shift occurred in the instant the new ability became yours. You became confident in this metamorphosis. The smallest shift in perspective can transform a life.

There is a profound distinction between the perceptions and beliefs around illness (our interpretations and stories that keep us stuck in no possibility), and the actual experience of living our later years on a daily basis (what actually happens). This distinction is these are separate phenomena and not viewed as one. New possibilities are created when we separate the phenomena. We step into freedom.

I have more difficulty with my hands in the hot, humid Philadelphia summer. My right hand is much less mobile than it used to be. I am forced to type with one finger. I have to eat exclusively with my left hand. My thumbs (which act as my legs when I accelerate my electric scooter) are stiffer and less predictable when I ask them to operate the scooter. My neurologist thinks that MS might be progressing. As I wrote this paragraph, I experienced a small amount of writer's block. I said to my assistant, "So what do I do now?" At that second, my phone rang. So she said, "You're going to answer the phone . . . with your hand." Of course!

The challenges with my hand have presented an opportunity for me to practice shifts in perception like those illustrated in this book. My neurologist's observation threw me into acceptance. I was forced to accept the reality of what is. I don't like it, but I've accepted it. And you can be sure I still get my nails done every week!

Look at *your* hands. What do you experience as you look at them? Do you only notice their color, wrinkles, age spots, or their other unique physical features? Or, do you think of what those hands have been through in your life, and how they have supported you? They have signed your name thousands of times, they have fed you, scratched your nose, gripped a bike handlebar or a tennis racquet, tied your shoes, gently touched the face of a loved one. Noticing or remembering all these things is your perception of your hands.

Now close your eyes and focus on your hands. Feel its tendons, muscles, bones—even the blood flowing in it. You may notice some tingling or vibration. You may notice some stiffness or pain. This is what your hands actually are *in the present moment*. But don't forget to acknowledge and thank your hands for being your friends.

Can you see or feel the difference between your perceptions of your hands and how your hands actually are *in the present moment*? It's the difference between reading a book about sailing and actually being on a sailboat.

Even though I am *physically* not able to do many things, I am spiritually free and capable of being a contributing, supporting, loving partner and friend. Of course, there are challenging moments, but I am able to separate what happens in my life because of illness or aging from a *story or interpretation* of what happens. I've discovered that much of what I've already determined may not be that way at all. I am not limited by a fixed set of options and alternatives, and I'm able to experience the joy of my relationship with joy and good humor. And this is another example of the power of shifting perception.

When a new disciple came to the Master, this is the catechism he was usually subjected to:
"Do you know the one person who will never abandon you in the whole of your lifetime?"
"Who is it?"
"You."
"And do you know the answer to every question you may have?"
"What is it?"
"You."
"And can you guess the solution to every one of your problems?"
"I give up."
"You."

-- Anthony de Mello, <u>One Minute Wisdom</u>

EPILOGUE:

Transformation of the Soul is through the Body

I n this book, you and I have been engaged in an exploration. And now that we have arrived at the final pages, I thank you for making this journey with me.

I hope that, for you, this will be where you begin to map out what the next stage of your life might be like.

I encourage you to be willing to be in the present—to accept life as it comes.

For me, Multiple Sclerosis was the universe's way to jolt me into a new place in my consciousness. For each one of us, challenges come in different forms. But whatever challenges we face, we must learn to expand with, and embrace, the life changes that come forward, instead of contracting, resisting, and rejecting them. *And we don't necessarily have to like it.*

So I invite you to take the next step. Move into that loving place where you can expand past any limitations and live in the freedom that is always within you. Consider that, beyond your body, mind, and emotions, there is a quieter place of stillness, completion, fulfillment, and wisdom. This place of unconditional loving and inner peace is more enduring and greater than any gift we could ever receive.

My wish for each of us is that we embrace the step-by-step process of a future worth living. This is what is so exciting about this journey—it never ends . . .

***

"Come to the edge," he said.
They said, "We are afraid."
"Come to the edge," he said.
They came.
He pushed them . . .
And they flew.

-- Guillaume Appollinaire

AFTERWORD
LOVING YOURSELF WELL

I'm Starting With The Man In
The Mirror,
I'm Asking Him To Change
His Ways
No Message Could Have
Been Any Clearer
(If You Wanna Make The
World A Better Place)
(Take A Look At Yourself And
Then Make The Change)
-- Michael Jackson

Throughout my first book, *You Are Not Your Illness,* I demonstrate to the reader that they are *not* their body, thoughts or emotions, but we are all *observers,* (or we become more aware) of our bodies, emotions, and thoughts.

Bear in mind that all of your relationships are inside you.

Ultimately each relationship you have with another person reflects your relationship you have with yourself. How well (or poorly) you get along with yourself will be directly mirrored by how quickly you come back to Self, to the centered space that abides within us all. You know, the part of us that is the still observer of our thoughts, emotions and experiences.

This may sound silly, but when was the last time you looked in the mirror at yourself and said, "I Love You."

We spend countless hours in front of the mirror reviewing our looks, focusing on our flaws and trying to create a perfect look...whatever that is. All of us are unique in our own right and *mirror work* gives us back that knowledge and wisdom.

What is mirror work? It's when you face yourself in the mirror, look into your eyes, and say, "I Love You." You may even tear up when you experience the magnificence of your true Self. You may be surprised how this simple process can have a profound affect on your well-being as its influence follows you throughout the day.

I do the following exercise daily. It grounds me and helps me gain back my personal power. Whenever I am in front of any mirror and say "I Love You Linda," a smile forms on my lips and my eyes start to twinkle. Physically, I start to experience changes within my body and it feels good when I breathe in deeply the love and appreciation I have for myself. Why wouldn't I want to feel happy?

Saying "I Love You" (put in your name) doesn't cost anything and we gain so much from this daily practice. Imagine saying, "I Love You" to yourself 10 times a day. What do you think will happen? You would start to love yourself even more than you do now.

Are you ready to give yourself some love today? Every time you are in front of a mirror, (especially when you wake up in the morning), say "I Love You (put in your name), I really, really love you", no matter what you first look like in the morning. It only takes a brief moment to nurture and support you. Wherever you are right now, you can do this.

If I have one wish for you, it is that you use the information and exercises in this book in such a way as to claim your own loving and a life filled with health, intimacy, and creative self-expression.

APPENDIX
Additional Quizzes and Exercises for Loving Yourself Well

GENERAL PERSONAL REVIEW/ASSESSMENT
Questions to think about:

- *How do you hold yourself back?*
- *Recall a time when you have done this.*
- *What beliefs and thoughts are you holding that limit you?*
- *What mistake are you afraid of making?*
- *What mistake have you made that you have not let go of?*
- *When you hold yourself back, in which part of your body do you feel tightness or imbalance?*
- *What needs to be loved right now?*
- *Place your hand over your heart and feel the loving going in and through your body.*
- *Forgive yourself for any judgments you are holding against yourself.*
- *Describe how you're feeling inside after this.*
- *What have you learned?*

PRACTICE and EXERCISE – CALM / STILLNESS

Most of what we struggle with is what we've added into the simple action of breathing in and breathing out. We've added our own expectations, desires, fears, insecurities, and projections. And if we're going to find any peace, we need take responsibility for our part in shaping our lives. *And our part is everything; we are responsible for it all—the good, the bad, and the ugly.*

Take a moment to call in and feel your Higher Power, no matter how you identify it (God, Nature, Spirit, etc.) Then think about an area of your life where you would like to be more CALM / STILL.

What is your *false self view* of this area of your life? Include all the ways in which you are judging, blaming, and seeing yourself as a victim of the situation.

Some examples of how *false self views* (worn out beliefs) affect our ability to be CALM/STILL:

- When our thoughts, feelings, words and actions are not in harmony, it shows up as imbalance, frustration, and anxiety.
- We may find it difficult to make rational, calm decision; we feel agitated, uncomfortable—something is off.
- We are out of balance: we think one thing, feel something else, say something different, and act in another way that has nothing to do with what we thought, felt, or said.
- When we disown part of ourselves through denial, self-judgment, or feeling victimized, we disempower ourselves emotionally and spiritually.

New Vision (*true self* views that can support us in being CALM/STILL):

- I must learn to love myself—not just the part I consider positive, but all of it: good, bad, light, dark; my strengths as well as my weaknesses. Self acceptance is essential to my health.
- I absorb and listen to the words I use; the actions that I take should be perfect reflections of the thoughts I think.
- I maintain this awareness; I'll notice when I am out of harmony and balance.

So, what do you do when you detect an imbalance? Pause, stop what you're about to say or do and investigate where the words/feelings are coming from. Most of the time, when we are agitated or stressed, it is a sign of disconnect or separation.

The true self's only game is the game of loving, which involves cooperation and caring.

When we look at life from a true self perspective, we continually discover new things about ourselves and others.

***

PRACTICE and EXERCISE – ACCEPTANCE

Think about an area of your life where you would like to be more **ACCEPTING.**

What is your *false self view* of this area of your life? Include all the ways in which you are judging, blaming, and seeing yourself as a victim of the situation.

Some examples of how *false self* views (worn out beliefs) affect our ability to be ACCEPTING:

- We react to mourning our losses by closing off our feelings from ourselves and each other, and resist feeling the pain of separation and the despair of loneliness.

- We often assume that sorrow, quiet desperation, and hopelessness go hand in hand with our diminishing physical or mental abilities and getting older.

Now come up with a *true self view* of this area of your life. Make a statement of ACCEPTANCE about what is going on for you in this area.

New Vision (*true self* views that can support us in being ACCEPTING):

- *I love myself unconditionally:* I love myself even though I feel uptight. I love myself even when I am pretending to be something I am not. I love myself even though I am judging. I love myself when I worry. I love myself even when I am being egotistical.
- As I accept my own life (and others' lives) *for what it is and for what it is not,* I recognize the reality of what it is, rather than fighting or judging it.
- I acknowledge and experience any feelings that may come up in the present moment.
- Since life is a series of situations and circumstances, I change how I feel about getting or not getting what I want.

When you're losing sleep, reviewing and worrying about a problem, it usually means you're not **accepting your situation**. Similarly, when you're upset with yourself, it generally means you aren't self-accepting. When you are judging yourself, you have strayed off the path to accepting yourself. This is the moment to reach for this guidebook.

***

PRACTICE and EXERCISE – COOPERATION

Think about an area of your life where you would like to be more **COOPERATIVE.**

What is your *false self view* of this area of your life? Include all the ways in which you are judging, blaming, and seeing yourself as a victim of the situation.

Some examples of how *false self views* (worn out beliefs) affect our ability to be COOPERATIVE:

- We resist letting go and need to prove to ourselves that we are better than others.
- We resist change and to not getting our way by accepting a new reality.
- We moan that life is unfair and we don't deserve bad things that happen to us.
- We blame God for not bringing greater happiness to us, which is blocking our cooperation.

Now come up with a *true self view* of this area of your life. Make a statement of COOPERATION about what is going on for you in this area.

New Vision (*true self* views that can support us in being COOPERATIVE):

- I shift my attitude to one of joy and enthusiasm for just being alive in the moment. I flow with what is present and see what I can learn from the situation.
- My focus extends beyond myself and my immediate needs and desires.
- I am always thinking, "What can I do for you that will assist you even more?"

***

PRACTICE and EXERCISE – COURAGE

Think about an area of your life where you would like to be more COURAGEOUS.

What is your *false self view* of this area of your life? Include all the ways in which you are judging, blaming, and seeing yourself as a victim of the situation.

Some examples of how *false self* views (worn out beliefs) affect our ability to be COURAGEOUS:

- It is easy to think of being in a wheelchair as being the "cause" of, or the excuse for, being unable to participate in activities or social occasions.
- We use phrases such as: we are unable to do what we "used to do," "could" have done, or "should" have done.
- We make decisions based on fear and variations of "something is wrong," or "I can't do it," or "I shouldn't do it," or "I'm not good enough."
- We are afraid because we feel the world will dismiss us and ultimately throw us away.

Now come up with your *true self view* of this area of your life. Make a statement of COURAGE about what is going on for you in this area.

New Vision (*true self* views that can support us in being COURAGEOUS):

- Courage is helpful in crisis, and is a fearless approach to living my life no matter my situation.
- It takes great courage to be in the present moment.
- The real reward of vulnerability is greater courage.
- I become strong by embracing my vulnerability.

You can deal with any challenge in this way: lovingly extend your energy field and encompass the situation, then maintain a mindset of neutral observation. This approach places you securely in your center, the Soul. Then, from this center, spiritual energy starts radiating outward. It does not radiate as personality, but as an expression of your Soul's light.

***

PRACTICE and EXERCISE – CONNECTION

Think about an area of your life where you would like to feel more **CONNECTED.**

What is your *false self view* of this area of your life? Include all the ways in which you are judging, blaming, and seeing yourself as a victim of the situation.

Some examples of *false self views* (worn out beliefs) that can affect our ability to feel CONNECTED:

- We cannot meet new friends, let alone a spouse or partner.
- Having the desire for human contact, romance and sex is too much trouble.
- We're afraid to promise anything to anybody… so we stay alone.
- We feel we've lost power to expect anything more for ourselves.
- Being in a wheelchair is sad and lonely.
- We yearn to feel heard, needed, and important.
- We seek validation and recognition in any available form.
- We limit our activities by clinging to our negative self-judgments. For example, we are afraid to ask old friends over for dinner because we must ask someone to cut up your food for us.

- We may think "I am not good enough," "I'm a burden to my friends," "I can't do it myself," or "I'm unworthy and do not like the attention."

Now come up with a *true self view* of this area of your life. Make a statement of
CONNECTION about what is going on for you in this area.

New Vision (*true self* views that can support us in being CONNECTED):

- I maintain a connection with the world, and mentor to a younger generation as they grow from adolescence into adulthood
- There are two parts to having a nourishing relationship: (1) empathy – sense what another person is feeling and understand what their intentions are, and (2) knowing how to listen, what to say, and how to time interactions so that I am effective and get what I want and need, and so does my partner.
- I stay engaged in life and keep things exciting, interesting and motivating.

***

PRACTICE and EXERCISE – GRATITUDE

Think about an area of your life where you would like to become more **GRATEFUL.**

What is your *false self view* of this area of your life? Include all the ways in which you are judging, blaming, and seeing yourself as a victim of the situation.

Some examples of *false self views* (worn out beliefs) that can affect our ability to feel GRATEFUL:

- We tend to feel entitled or special, because we are in a wheelchair.
- We may be unwilling to stay in the present moment, even though we know it is the only moment there is.

Now come up with your *true self view* of this area of your life. Make a statement of GRATITUDE about what is going on for you in this area.

New Vision (*true self* views that can support us in being GRATEFUL):

- Gratitude reminds me to find my happiness in everything—in exceptional things, in mundane things, in good things, in so-so things, and even in terrible things.
- I appreciate all that is so magnificent (or not so magnificent) in my life—my relationships, my family, my life's work, my finances, my retirement plans, my country, my faith, etc.
- Gratitude is a fully awake reminder of a loving, higher power within.
- When I am feeling thankful, I can be more receptive to making a difference in my world.

The above exercises for the road map markers of Calm/Stillness, Acceptance, Cooperation, Courage, Connection, and Gratitude can be adapted for the remaining markers. I encourage you to continue with the other markers (Understanding, Forgiveness, Enthusiasm, Creativity, Creative Thinking, Giving Back, Freedom, and Transformation), following the steps of thinking of an area of your life where you would like to be more self-supportive, noting false self views and true self views. This will support you in the remainder of the journey through the road map and beyond. May you continue to love yourself well.

***

PRACTICE: OBSERVING YOUR BREATH

It is important to be able to bring your full attention to the present moment. Your breath can assist you in this. By simply observing your breathing, you can bring yourself to a receptive and relaxed state in a very short time.

Try this:

- Close your eyes and focus on the rising and falling of your breath for 10 seconds.

- Let your awareness expand beyond your body to fill the space you are in.

- Experience yourself being held by that space. Lean forward a little and feel the support. Then lean back a little back and again feel the space hold you.

- Your mind and your emotions are being held by this space in a similar way.

- As you become attuned to your body, mind and emotions being held by this space, you will feel more confident about letting go of bodily tension, emotional worry, and mental preoccupations.

- Now bring that sense of space inside you. Sometimes it will seem like a bubble of clear light. Throughout the day, as you maintain awareness of this sacred space, you will start to feel relaxed and centered.

- It is easy to give the space away to a negative thought, a distraction, a stressful event, or getting someone's approval. When that happens, simply bring yourself back to this sacred space by reminding yourself that you are loved.

- As you continue to work with this practice, you will begin to observe how you give your center away. Perhaps you allow yourself to be ruffled by a slow-moving line at the airport, a traffic jam, a disagreement with your spouse or healthcare aide, or misplacing your car keys when you're late for an appointment.

- **When you feel frustrated, ask yourself:** *Is this really worth losing my peace of mind and compromising my health and well-being?*

- As you become more attuned to the sacred space within, you will become less and less inclined to give it up to passing thoughts or irrelevant distractions.

- Remaining calm and relaxed will no longer be a matter of discipline; it will be a pleasure. **Being with your true self will be your highest priority.**

Have compassion for yourself by looking for the good and the divine in people and things. Leave the rest to a Higher Power.

Thank you for having the courage to love yourself enough to 'walk' this path with me.

Warmly, Linda

Three men carrying me down the path to the city of Aswan

We realize that wheelchairs and walkers and broken bodies are not who we are, that who we are is about fortitude and resilience and love of life.

—from the foreword by Dr. Daniel Gottlieb

Author Contact

Linda Noble Topf
www.wheelchairwisdom.com
484-434-8020 office
610-405-1815 cell

Linda Noble Topf is the author of *You Are Not your Illness: Seven Principles for Meeting the Challenge*, which shows that illness, injury, or disability can not only physically alter the course of your life, but can also cause great emotional upheaval and loss of self-worth. In this remarkable and uplifting book, Linda delves deeply into her own experience to share with readers the keys to regaining emotional and spiritual wholeness. Linda believes that real healing has nothing to do with the state of the physical body, and she offers a compassionate and inspirational message—along with support, skills, and encouragement—to those who want to embrace the challenge of living successfully with illness. It is her intention to leave people transformed with more power, freedom, self expression, and peace of mind.

Linda's second book, *Wheelchair Wisdom™: Awaken Your Spirit through Adversity*, shatters widespread notions of what it's like to spend life in a wheelchair, which addresses the unique circumstances of the millions of people in wheelchairs. She wants to convey the message that lies at the heart of her convictions—that people are more than their wheelchairs, more than their disabled bodies. Wheelchair Wisdom™ bears testimony to what Linda has learned and experienced—that each of us, regardless of circumstances, can move through life with freedom in a creative and joyful way.

Books in print, digital and audio formats are found at Amazon.com

Open Book Editions
A Berrett-Koehler Partner

Open Book Editions is a joint venture between Berrett-Koehler Publishers and Author Solutions, the market leader in self-publishing. There are many more aspiring authors who share Berrett-Koehler's mission than we can sustainably publish. To serve these authors, Open Book Editions offers a comprehensive self-publishing opportunity.

A Shared Mission

Open Book Editions welcomes authors who share the Berrett-Koehler mission—Creating a World That Works for All. We believe that to truly create a better world, action is needed at all levels—individual, organizational, and societal. At the individual level, our publications help people align their lives with their values and with their aspirations for a better world. At the organizational level, we promote progressive leadership and management practices, socially responsible approaches to business, and humane and effective organizations. At the societal level, we publish content that advances social and economic justice, shared prosperity, sustainability, and new solutions to national and global issues.

Open Book Editions represents a new way to further the BK mission and expand our community. We look forward to helping more authors challenge conventional thinking, introduce new ideas, and foster positive change.

For more information, see the Open Book Editions website:
http://www.iuniverse.com/Packages/OpenBookEditions.aspx

Join the BK Community! See exclusive author videos, join discussion groups, find out about upcoming events, read author blogs, and much more! http://bkcommunity.com/

Printed in the United States
By Bookmasters